THEMATIC UNIT
Electricity

Written by Kathee Gosnell

Teacher Created Materials, Inc.
6421 Industry Way
Westminster, CA 92683
www.teachercreated.com

ISBN-1-55734-236-9

©1994 Teacher Created Materials, Inc.
Reprinted, 1999
Updated, 2000
Made in U.S.A.

Illustrated by

Keith Vasconcelles

Edited by

Karen J. Goldfluss

Cover Art by

Theresa M. Wright

Table of Contents

Introduction

Electricity contains a captivating, whole language, thematic unit about the discovery, development, and uses of electricity. Its 80 exciting pages are filled with a wide variety of lesson ideas and reproducible pages designed for use with intermediate children. Activities are included which set the stage for reading, encourage the enjoyment of the book, and extend the concepts gained. In addition, the theme is connected to the curriculum with activities in language arts, math, science, social studies, art, and life skills. Many of these activities encourage cooperative learning. Suggestions and patterns for bulletin board and unit management tools are additional time savers for the busy teacher. Highlighting this complete teacher resource are two culminating activities: "A Day Without Electricity" and "Electricity Fair." These activities allow students to synthesize and apply their knowledge beyond the classroom.

This thematic unit includes the following:

☐ **Literature selections**—summaries of two children's books with related lessons (complete with reproducible pages) that cross the curriculum

☐ **Planning Guides**—suggestions for sequencing lessons each day of the unit

☐ **Writing Ideas**—daily suggestions, including big books, for writing across the curriculum

☐ **Curriculum connections**—activities in language arts, math, science, social studies, art, and life skills

☐ **Group projects**—activities to foster cooperative learning

☐ **Bulletin board ideas**—suggestions and plans for student-created and/or interactive bulletin boards

☐ **Culminating activities**—ideas which require students to synthesize their learning by engaging in an activity that can be shared by others

☐ **A bibliography**—a list suggesting additional literature books on the theme

---

To keep this valuable resource intact so it can be used year after year, you may wish to punch holes in the pages and store them in a three-ring binder.

Introduction *(cont.)*

Why a Balanced Approach?

The strength of a whole language approach is that it involves children in using all modes of communication—reading, writing, listening, illustrating, and doing. Communication skills are interconnected and integrated into lessons that emphasize the whole of language. Balancing this approach is our knowledge that every whole—including individual words—is composed of parts, and directed study of those parts can help a student to master the whole. Experience and research tell us that regular attention to phonics, other word attack skills, spelling, etc., develops reading mastery, thereby fulfilling the unity of the whole language experience. The child is thus led to read, write, spell, speak, and listen confidently in response to a literature experience introduced by the teacher. In these ways, language skills grow rapidly, stimulated by direct practice, involvement, and interest in the topic at hand.

Why Thematic Planning?

One very useful tool for implementing a balanced language program is thematic planning. By choosing a theme with correlating literature selections for a unit of study, a teacher can plan activities throughout the day that lead to a cohesive, in-depth study of the topic. Students will be practicing and applying their skills in meaningful contexts. Consequently, they will tend to learn and retain more. Both teachers and students will be freed from a day that is broken into unrelated segments of isolated drill and practice.

Why Cooperative Learning?

Besides academic skills and content, students need to learn social skills. This area of development cannot be taken for granted. Students must learn to work cooperatively in groups in order to function well in modern society. Group activities should be a regular part of school life, and teachers should consciously include social objectives as well as academic objectives in their planning. For example, a group working together to solve a problem may need to select a leader. Teachers should make clear to the students the qualities of good leader-follower group interaction just as they would state and monitor the academic goals of the project.

Why Internet Extenders?

Internet extenders have been added to many of the activities in this book to enhance them through quality Web sites. This supplemental information helps to expand the students' knowledge of the topic, as well as make them aware of the many valuable resources to be found on the Internet. Some Web sites lend themselves to group research; other sites are best viewed by the entire class. If one is available, use a large-screen monitor when the entire class is viewing the Web site and discussing its content.

Although these Web sites have been carefully selected, they may not exist forever. Teacher Created Materials attempts to offset the ongoing problem of sites which move, "go dark" or otherwise leave the Internet after a book has been printed. If you attempt to contact a Web site listed in this unit and find that it no longer exists, check the TCM home page at www.teachercreated.com for updated URL's for this book.

Inventors and Their Inventions

Summary

It has been said that Thomas Alva Edison was the greatest inventor of his time. He helped bring electricity to the world. However, there were other great scientists and inventors working to find ways to improve the quality of life. This section of *Electricity* introduces students to the following inventors: Thomas Alva Edison, Lewis Howard Latimer, Michael Faraday, Samuel F. B. Morse, and Alexander Graham Bell. Their inventions furthered the development and use of electricity. With the development of electricity, technology shifted into high gear.

The outline below is a suggested plan for using the various activities that are presented in this unit. You should adapt these ideas to fit your own classroom situation.

Sample Plan

Day 1

- Read and discuss the biography of Thomas Alva Edison. (page 9)
- Fill in Language Arts "Crossword Puzzle." (page 36)
- Learn scientific background with "Great Discoveries in Electricity." (pages 55–59)

Day 2

- Read and discuss the biography of Lewis H. Latimer. (page 10)
- Introduce "Daily Writing Topics." (pages 28 and 29)
- Read "Thinking Like a Scientist." (page 45)
- Begin student-created books. (pages 30–34)
- Identify electrical conductors. (page 48)

Day 3

- Read and discuss the biography of Michael Faraday. (page 11)
- Create Morse "Copy Art." (page 62)
- Continue "Daily Writing Topics." (pages 28 and 29)
- Learn the Morse Code. (page 37)
- Solve "Electricity Facts" problems. (page 38)
- Experiment with rheostats. (page 44)

Day 4

- Read and discuss the biography of Samuel F. B. Morse. (page 12)
- Continue "Daily Writing Topics." (pages 28 and 29)
- Build a telegraph set. (page 51)
- Write a "Scientific Journal Magazine Article." (page 15)
- Learn how to be a meter reader. (page 39)
- Continue student-created books. (pages 30–34)

Day 5

- Read and discuss the biography of Alexander Graham Bell. (page 13)
- Continue "Daily Writing Topics." (pages 28 and 29)
- Practice cause-effect relationships. (page 14)
- Calculate household electricity usage. (page 40)
- Design a modern home. (page 63)

Day 6

- Continue "Daily Writing Topics." (pages 28 and 29)
- Experience "A Day Without Electricity." (page 67)
- Build a motor. (page 47)
- Create "Electrical Parts Art." (page 62)
- Learn about careers in the electricity field. (page 64)
- Prepare for "Electricity Fair." (page 68–72)

Overview of Activities

1. Prepare your classroom for a unit on electricity. Collect books, magazines, and pamphlets on Thomas Edison and other inventors and scientists listed in the Word Bank on page 35 and Bibliography on page 79. Collect and display resources on the topic of electricity, power plants, energy sources, etc.

2. Ask students to bring in old radios, electric clocks, small motors, etc., that no longer work. Create a "Touch Table" for students to examine and take apart the electrical mechanisms.

3. Brainstorm with the students to see how much they know about electricity. Prepare a chart on a large piece of paper and ask students to share their ideas about electricity while you write them down. Display the chart. At the end of the thematic unit, have students evaluate what they have learned by comparing their knowledge about electricity before and after the unit.

4. Introduce students to the unit by reading Thomas Alva Edison's biography on page 9. Point out to students that although he is the most famous inventor associated with electricity, he is not the only individual who contributed inventions in this field. Remind them that they will learn about other inventors and their inventions in this unit. Encourage students to locate and share as much information about electricity and inventions related to it as possible.

5. Discuss with the class what life was like before electricity. Ask students to imagine what their lives would be like, how school would be different, etc., without electricity.

6. Introduce students to the terminology, history, inventors, and scientists in the field of electricity. Have students complete the crossword puzzle on page 36. Prepare the "Great Discoveries in Electricity" activity on pages 55–59. Then, have groups of students play the game and/or make time lines.

7. Distribute copies of the "Safety Rules" on page 77 and discuss the importance of handling electrical devices responsibly.

8. Have students read the biography of Lewis Howard Latimer on page 10. They will learn that, among his inventions, Latimer developed a long-lasting filament that revolutionized electric lighting. Discuss the events and accomplishments of his life and his contributions to science.

Management

Safety Rules

Experimenting with electricity can be lots of fun, but if used improperly or carelessly, electricity can be very dangerous. Here are some important rules to remember when working around or with electricity. Read and discuss them with your friends and family. Then, add your own safety rules about electricity.

- Never touch an electrical appliance or switch with wet hands.
- Before plugging or unplugging an electrical appliance, make sure the power is turned off.
- When connecting or disconnecting an electrical device, be sure it is unplugged.
- If an electrical cord is worn, do not use it. Tell an adult that it needs to be replaced.
- Do not overload a circuit by plugging in too many electrical appliances at one time.
- Remove the batteries from toys and games when they are not being used for a long time. An old, corroded battery left in a toy or game can destroy it.
- Do not touch a bare wire.
- Never handle an electrical appliance, switch, telephone set, or radio while in the bathtub.

© Teacher Created Materials, Inc.   77   #236 Thematic Unit—Electricity

Overview of Activities *(cont.)*

9. Introduce "Daily Writing Topics" (pages 28 and 29). You may wish to have students include the activities in this unit as part of an existing writing journal or ask students to prepare a folder in which to keep their related writing activities for "Electricity."

10. Discuss the importance of the telegraph to the work of Thomas Edison and other inventors involved in the study of electricity. Read and discuss the biography of Samuel F. B. Morse on page 12. Have students complete the Morse "Copy Art" project (page 62) and "Get the Message" (page 37). Divide the class into small groups and have each group build a telegraph set. Directions on how to build and use the telegraph are provided on page 51. Have groups practice sending and interpreting telegraph messages.

11. Discuss the difficulties encountered by Edison and other inventors. Discuss why it is important to record failures as well as successes. Read "Thinking Like a Scientist" (page 45) with students. Have students use the scientific method to experiment with "Material Conductors" (page 48) and to complete the experiment form on page 46. If students have not had experience with this procedure, you may need to model the activity.

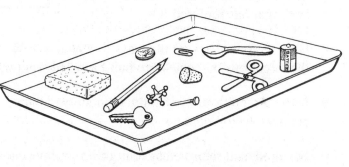

12. It has been said that with the invention of the telephone, the world became a little smaller. Discuss the meaning of this statement with your students. Have students name other inventions that have "shrunk the world," such as the steamship, the airplane, etc.

    Read and discuss the biography of Alexander Graham Bell (page 13). If possible, invite a speaking deaf person to the classroom to talk to the students. Discuss how Mr. Bell became interested in working with the deaf and how this led to the invention of the telephone. Discuss Thomas Edison's improvements on the "speaking telegraph."

13. Thomas Edison was greatly influenced by Michael Faraday's pioneer work in electricity. Have students read the biography of Michael Faraday. Model the "Bright Ideas" cause-effect activity on page 14. Have students prepare a similar diagram for Alexander Graham Bell, Michael Faraday, or Samuel F. B. Morse. Ask students to share their ideas with the class.

14. Students will learn interesting facts about electricity as they solve problems with "Electricity Facts" (page 38). As an extension, have students work in groups to research additional facts and prepare their own "Electricity Facts" problems.

15. Provide students with everyday experiences on the many uses of electricity. Provide materials on reading electric meters and determining monthly electric bills. Have students work individually or in groups to complete "Be a Meter Reader" (page 39), "What's the Charge?" (page 40), and "Shedding Light on the Subject" (page 44).

Overview of Activities *(cont.)*

16. Encourage students to create their own books about electricity. Use some of the suggestions on pages 30–34. Display student-created books at a writing center. Prepare a library sign-up system in the class for students to check out books from the center.

17. The telegraph was one of the greatest inventions of the mid-19th century, yet today it is all but forgotten. Have students research and discuss the uses of the telegraph in the local community and throughout the world. If the telegraph is no longer in use, find out why this came about and what has replaced it.

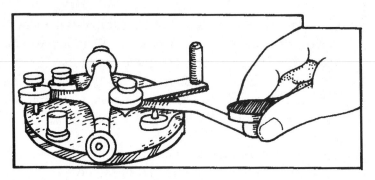

18. Have students explore the ways in which electricity is used to produce power and motion. Follow the directions on page 47 to build a simple motor.

19. Invite a representative from the phone company into your classroom to speak about the telephone and its development.

20. Divide the classroom into four groups. Have each group represent one of the following inventors: Lewis Howard Latimer, Michael Faraday, Alexander Graham Bell, Samuel F. B. Morse. Ask student groups to brainstorm ideas as to why their inventor was the most influential person in Edison's life and inventions. Have each group choose a spokesperson and have a mock debate. Have them use notes prepared during the brainstorming sessions. Whenever possible, back up statements, using quotes from books, encyclopedias, or other resources. Allow ample time for research.

21. Divide students into groups and assign each group a different inventor to research, using Web sites described in Inventors on the Internet (page 15). Have one member from each group impersonate the inventor, telling of his life and invention in story format to the rest of the class.

22. Create sculptures from electrical parts. Start a classroom collection of electrical materials and have students build "Electrical Parts Art" (page 62).

23. Encourage students to design the interior of a modern home to include furnishing and electrical appliances. Use the floor plan on page 63. Have students share their ideas with the class.

24. Experience "A Day Without Electricity" (page 67). Have students share their thoughts about their experiences without electricity for a period of time. Begin preparing for the "Electricity Fair." Suggestions and culminating projects are provided on pages 68–72.

Thomas Alva Edison

When Thomas Alva Edison's schoolteacher told his mother that he was "addled" (easily confused), Mrs. Edison took him out of school. Young Edison turned to books for his education. Not only could he read quickly, but he could remember almost everything he read.

After reading books on science, Thomas built a chemical laboratory in his house. When he needed money for materials, he got a job as a newspaper carrier on a train. Soon he was able to buy secondhand printing equipment and began publishing a newspaper of his own.

Next, he set up a lab in the baggage car, but an unfortunate chemical fire got him and his equipment thrown off the train. During another train accident, he was pulled to safety by his ears, which resulted in permanent damage to his hearing.

When Edison was 23, he founded the first firm of consulting engineers. For the next six years, he turned out a number of inventions. In 1876, he set up a laboratory in Menlo Park, New Jersey. This became the first industrial research laboratory. Thomas Edison's goal was to produce a new invention every 10 days. During one four-year stretch, he obtained 300 patents—one for every five days! In his lifetime, he patented 1,100 inventions.

Some of Edison's inventions include the phonograph, the electric light bulb, the movie camera, and the stock ticker. All of these devices have been transformed over the years into more modern, usable forms. Thanks to the genius of Thomas Alva Edison, the world has literally been transformed into a brighter place! Edison died at the age of 84 on October 18, 1932, the fifty-second anniversary of the light bulb.

Lewis Howard Latimer

Ask anyone who invented the electric light bulb, and they are sure to answer that is was Thomas Alva Edison. Few people realize that Lewis Howard Latimer played a large part in the development of this invention. Mr. Latimer was able to produce a long-lasting filament for the bulbs. This filament would help revolutionize electric lighting.

Lewis Latimer was born in 1848. As the son of fugitive slaves, he had a very hard life. It was not until his discharge from the Union navy, when he went to work as a clerk for patent lawyers, that Lewis Latimer became interested in the invention drawings prepared by draftsmen. Latimer saved enough money to buy some used drafting equipment and books and then taught himself to duplicate their work. By 1874, he received his first patent; he had co-invented an improved water closet in use on trains. Later, he was to meet Alexander Graham Bell, for whom he completed designs for the telephone.

In 1880, Latimer joined inventor Hiram Maxim's U.S. Electric Lighting Company, where he developed a long-lasting filament and patented an improved electric lamp and an electric lamp socket. Four years later, in 1884, he went to work for Thomas Edison, who recognized his potential in the electrical field. Edison was not disappointed. No only did Latimer help the Edison Electric Light Company win its legal battles against Maxim, but he also served as a draftsman in the engineering department. Later he was named the company's chief draftsman and patent expert.

Over the years Latimer continued to develop his own inventions. They included a safety elevator; electric fireworks; a locking rack for coats, hats, and umbrellas; and a book supporter for books on shelves. His greatest honor came, though, when he became a charter member of the Edison Pioneers, an organization made up of the men who had created the electrical industry. He continued to work in the electrical field until 1924. Four years later, Latimer died at his home in New York.

Michael Faraday

Michael Faraday was an English physicist. A physicist is someone who studies the science of matter (anything that occupies space and has weight) and energy (the ability of matter to move or chemically change other matter) and how they are related. He was also a chemist (someone who studies the composition, structure, properties, and reactions of matter).

Faraday was born in Newington, England, on September 22, 1791. He died in Hampton Court, England, on August 25, 1867. He was one of the greatest experimental scientists of all time, even though he had a poor education and no university training. He discovered that electricity and magnetism are related. This was an important step in making electricity useful to people.

In 1813, Faraday began his scientific work as an assistant to the English scientist Sir Humphrey Davy at the Royal Society of London for the Advancement of Science. He worked there until he retired in 1858.

His first important discovery was in 1821. He discovered that a magnetic field is created around a wire carrying electric current.

In 1831, he reproduced electricity from magnetic forces. He showed that when a wire is moved through the field of a magnet, an electric current is generated in the wire.

The set of books that contained the works of Michael Faraday was bought by Thomas Edison. He was so fascinated by Faraday's pioneer work in electricity that he would read for hours and hours. Thomas Edison refused to sleep and barely ate. Needless to say, Faraday had a great influence on Thomas Edison and his electrical experiments and inventions.

Samuel F. B. Morse

Samuel Finley Breese Morse was born in Charlestown, Massachusetts, on April 27, 1791. He died in New York City, New York, on April 2, 1872. Morse was the main inventor of the telegraph. With the invention of the telegraph, it became possible to transmit information to distant parts of the country (as long as there were telegraph lines available) in just minutes. Before the telegraph, it had taken hours, days, or even weeks to send messages between cities.

Although Samuel Morse is most famous as an inventor of the telegraph, his first interest was art. He graduated from Yale College in 1810. He became known both as a painter and a sculptor, but he did not earn very much money.

In 1832, Morse began working on the telegraph. He didn't have much technical knowledge, so he needed to seek device from his friend Leonard Gale and from a leading American scientist, Joseph Henry.

Morse's first telegraph receiver, built in 1835, was very different from the final form of the instrument. It used a pen to transcribe (copy in writing) a code onto a moving strip of paper. Later, he invented the sounder which sent the code by means of clicks, a short click was a dot and a longer click was a dash. Two other important inventions made by Samuel Morse were the Morse Code (see page 37) and the telegraph relay, which made telegraphy possible over long distances.

On May 24, 1844, Morse telegraphed a message over a trial telegraph line from Washington, D.C., to Baltimore, Maryland. The famous message said: "What hath God wrought!"

12

Alexander Graham Bell

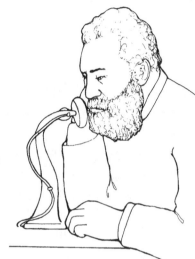

Alexander Graham Bell was born in Edinburgh, Scotland, in 1847. Bell's father was a professor of speech at the University of Edinburgh. Because Mrs. Bell was partly deaf, the whole family was interested in speech and sounds of all kinds. By experimenting, they studied how sounds are made and how they are carried from one place to another. The Bells moved to Canada in 1870 after the death of Alexander's brother—hoping that Alexander would become stronger in the fresh Canadian air. In Canada, Alexander became a teacher of the deaf. He was such a good teacher that others tried to learn his methods of teaching. He moved to the United States where he became a professor at Boston University.

Mr. Bell met a young electrician by the name of Thomas Watson. Together they worked to find the way to send a voice over wires. They had many disappointing failures. Then one day in June of 1875, Watson, who was two floors below, heard Bell's voice from the attic: "Mr. Watson, please come here. I want you." Watson had clearly heard Bell over the wire they were experimenting with.

At first people thought that the telephone was just a toy. They didn't believe it would be useful. In time, the telephone became recognized as a wonderful invention. As part of the Centennial Exposition of 1876 in Philadelphia, Alexander Graham Bell's invention of the telephone received the Exposition Medal. In 1877, a telephone company was formed. The first telephone exchange was opened in 1878 in New Haven, Connecticut. The exchange had 8 lines and 21 telephones. Two years later, there were over 47,000 telephones in the United States.

Bright Ideas

Thomas Edison was a proponent of the use of visual representation as is evidenced by the following quote: "Suppose . . . we show the child . . . the cocoon unfolding, the butterfly actually emerging. The knowledge which comes from the actual seeing is worthwhile."

Use the following activity to help students think critically about the effect that Edison's inventions had on the world. By making a visual representation of the connections between the inventions and their effects upon the world, the students can more easily understand cause and effect.

Directions

1. On a chalkboard or overhead projector, draw a light bulb diagram similar to the one on this page.
2. Choose an Edison invention or a contribution to an invention from the Word Bank on page 35. This will be a cause.
3. Direct the students to suggest possible effects on people and events in history. Record them on "wires" connected to the light bulb.
4. Have students work individually or in small groups to brainstorm more "Bright Ideas" that connect an invention or contribution to its effects. Have students create a cause-effect diagram on light-colored construction paper. Display the completed diagrams on a wall or bulletin board.

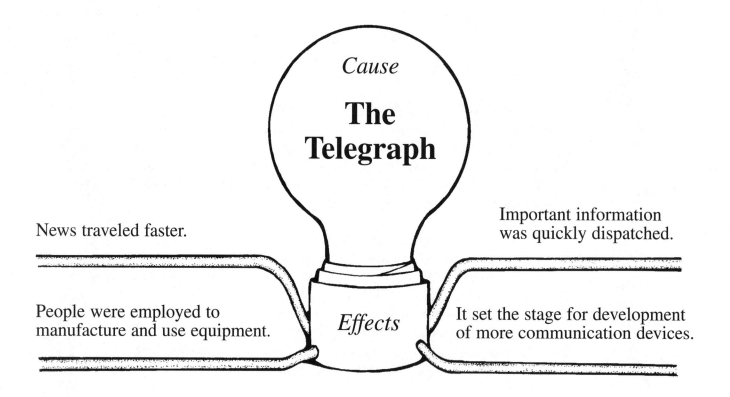

Extension

Have students prepare similar visual representations for other inventors and the inventions they created in the field of electricity.

Inventors on the Internet

Directions: Divide the students into groups and assign each group a different inventor to research, using the Web sites described below. Have one member from each group impersonate the inventor, telling of his life and invention in story format to the rest of the class.

Thomas Edison

http://www.edisonian.com/

http://memory.loc.gov/ammem/edhtml/

Activity Summary: The first Web site provides information about Edison's life and inventions. A time line of Edison's life is given at the last Web site, along with examples of Edison's work in making moving pictures, which can be viewed if you have the QuickTime plugin.

Lewis Howard Latimer

http://www.energy.ca.gov/education/scientists/latimer.html

Activity Summary: A brief biography of Lewis Latimer is provided here, as well as a photograph. Follow the link at this Web site to learn more about this scientist.

Michael Faraday

http://www.energy.ca.gov/education/scientists/faraday.html

http://www.spartacus.schoolnet.co.uk/Scfaraday.htm

Activity Summary: Read a brief biography of Faraday at both Web sites. The latter shows a photograph of the scientist. The former has a link to an article about Faraday, written by electrical engineers.

Samuel F. B. Morse

http://www.morsehistoricsite.org/morse/morse.html

Activity Summary: Read an excellent biography of this scientist at this Web site.

Alexander Graham Bell

http://www.fitzgeraldstudio.com/html/bell/default.html

Activity Summary: This Web site has extensive background on Bell. Follow the links to learn about his inventions, including the telephone, kites, and planes.

Philo Farnsworth

http://web.mit.edu/invent/www/inventorsA-H/farnsworth.html

Activity Summary: Read this interesting biography of the man who, at age 15, invented television.

Henry Ford

http://web.mit.edu/inventwww/inventorsA-H/ford.html

Activity Summary: Read a brief biography of the man who invented the assembly line for rapid production of automobiles.

Benjamin Franklin

http://web.mit.edu/invent/www/inventorsA-H/franklin.html

Activity Summary: This biography of one of the founders of our nation gives great insight into his life as an inventor. Follow the links to learn more about this fascinating man.

Electricity

by Steve Parker

Summary

With Benjamin Franklin's lightning experiments, the Age of Electricity began the task of harnessing energy into a controllable unit of power. *Electricity* is a valuable resource that will enlighten students about inventions that store, produce, and use electricity. Today, electric power is something most people take for granted. The information presented in *Electricity* demonstrates to students the role of electricity as an energy source in the past, present, and future.

The outline below is a suggested plan for using the various activities that are presented in this unit. You should adapt these ideas to fit your own classroom situation.

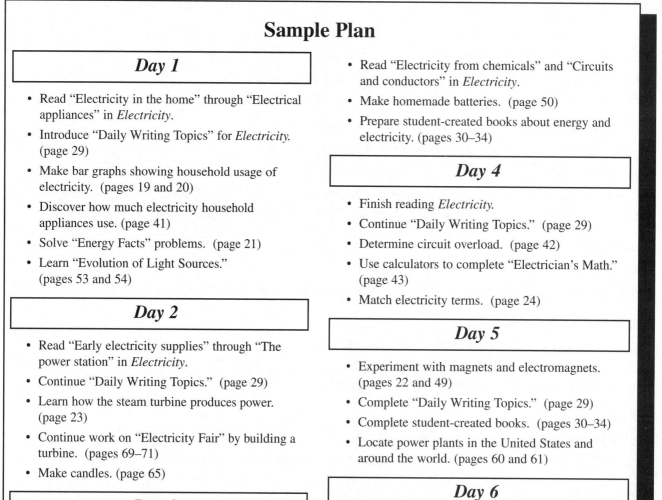

Sample Plan

Day 1

- Read "Electricity in the home" through "Electrical appliances" in *Electricity*.
- Introduce "Daily Writing Topics" for *Electricity*. (page 29)
- Make bar graphs showing household usage of electricity. (pages 19 and 20)
- Discover how much electricity household appliances use. (page 41)
- Solve "Energy Facts" problems. (page 21)
- Learn "Evolution of Light Sources." (pages 53 and 54)

Day 2

- Read "Early electricity supplies" through "The power station" in *Electricity*.
- Continue "Daily Writing Topics." (page 29)
- Learn how the steam turbine produces power. (page 23)
- Continue work on "Electricity Fair" by building a turbine. (pages 69–71)
- Make candles. (page 65)

Day 3

- Read "The quest for knowledge" through "Using charges" in *Electricity*.
- Continue "Daily Writing Topics." (page 29)
- Experiment with static electricity. (pages 25 and 26)

- Read "Electricity from chemicals" and "Circuits and conductors" in *Electricity*.
- Make homemade batteries. (page 50)
- Prepare student-created books about energy and electricity. (pages 30–34)

Day 4

- Finish reading *Electricity*.
- Continue "Daily Writing Topics." (page 29)
- Determine circuit overload. (page 42)
- Use calculators to complete "Electrician's Math." (page 43)
- Match electricity terms. (page 24)

Day 5

- Experiment with magnets and electromagnets. (pages 22 and 49)
- Complete "Daily Writing Topics." (page 29)
- Complete student-created books. (pages 30–34)
- Locate power plants in the United States and around the world. (pages 60 and 61)

Day 6

- Discover how electricity behaves in presence of water. (page 52)
- Have a mock public hearing. (page 66)
- Compare energy sources. (page 27)
- Make an electricity montage. (page 62)
- Complete "Electricity Fair." (page 68)

Overview of Activities

Setting the Stage

---

1. Introduce "Daily Writing Topics" for *Electricity* (page 29). Have students include their writing activities in a writing journal or folder.

2. Prepare the "We're Getting Brighter" bulletin board on page 73. Make a pictograph to show the number of biographies the students have read about inventors and scientists whose work influenced the field of electricity.

3. Invite a representative from your local power company to discuss how electricity is brought to homes, schools, businesses, etc. Ask guest speakers to discuss the various careers at the power company and the training/education required to perform the various jobs. If possible, provide visual representation, such as models, pictures, diagrams, etc., that would enhance students' understanding of the power company's role in the community.

4. Distribute "Electricity—A Household Word" (page 19). Have students complete page 19 at home. Ask students to fill in the bar graph on page 20, using the information they collected from page 19. Discuss the students' bar graphs in terms of household usage of electrical appliances.

5. Have students complete the "Energy Facts" problems on page 21. The solutions provide facts about energy. Write the completed facts on a large piece of paper and display them on a wall. Refer to them as you read *Electricity*. Add new facts as each chapter of the book is read.

6. Introduce students to light sources that were used prior to the incandescent light bulb. Discuss the problems associated with each light source. Distribute copies of pages 53 and 54. Have students locate information on the various light sources and make a time line to show when each light source was most widely used.

Enjoying the Book

---

1. Read and discuss "The quest for knowledge" through "Using charges" in *Electricity*. Explain to the class that there are two kinds of electricity—static electricity and current electricity. Static electricity is produced by friction and can be easily reproduced by students. Distribute copies of pages 25 and 26 and let students try the experiments.

2. Read "Electricity from chemicals" and "Circuits and conductors." Then make the "Homemade Batteries" described on page 50. Discuss how batteries are used to produce current electricity. Talk about the role of electricity in the production of power and energy.

3. Divide the class into groups. Explain that they will build a device (turbine) that helps produce electricity. Discuss power plants. Ask students how they think electricity can be generated and how it gets to our homes, business, etc. Using the materials, directions, and explanations on pages 69–71, allow student groups to build their turbines. Discuss how the turbine turns to power an electrical generator and how the generator works to produce electricity from the energy of a moving magnetic field. Display the turbines at the Electricity Fair. (See page 68).

4. Discuss the invention of the steam turbine as a source of power used to run machinery. Have students complete the activity on page 23. Collect and display pictures of machines that use steam turbines as their power sources. Discuss the use of fossil fuels.

Overview of Activities *(cont.)*

Enjoying the Book (cont.)

5. Read and discuss "Early electricity supplies" through "The power station" in *Electricity*. Discuss the uses of fossil fuels (coal, oil, and natural gas), solar energy, and nuclear energy as sources of power. Divide the class into 5 groups. Ask each group to research one of the sources and present to the class information on the benefits and problems associated with its use. Reproduce the Venn diagram on page 27 and have students compare and contrast various energy sources.

6. Read and discuss "Electricity in the home" through "Electrical Appliances" in *Electricity*. Display pictures of household electrical appliances. Ask students how much electricity they think is used (a lot, some, very little) by each of the appliances. Distribute copies of page 41. Define *ampere, watt,* and *volt*. Have students find the amperes of electricity for the listed items.

7. Read "Resisting electricity" through "Magnetism from electricity" in *Electricity*. Discuss what happens when a wire carries more electricity than it should. Have students complete the activity on page 42 to determine which circuits are safe and which ones may be overloaded. Distribute copies of page 43 to students. Using calculators, ask students to apply the formulas and the information in the chart to which household items can be used on a 15 ampere circuit.

8. Read and discuss "Electromagnets." Divide the class into small groups. Provide each group with copies of the magnet and electromagnet experiments on pages 22 and 49, and the experiment form on page 46. Have student groups perform the experiments and discuss their observations and results with each other.

Extending the Book

1. Read "Discoveries using electricity (Electroplating)". Extend students' understanding of electrical conductivity with the experiment on page 52. Discuss how the addition of salt affects the results of the experiment. Electroplating is the production of a metal coating on a substance by means of electricity. Have students research the uses of electroplating. If possible, conduct classroom experiments with copperplating.

2. If possible, take a trip to your local power plant, hydroelectric dam, or utility station.

3. Distribute copies of the maps on pages 60 and 61. Have students locate and label the major nuclear and/or hydroelectric power plants. Ask students to suggest reasons for the plants' locations.

4. Discuss the need for public hearings. Divide the class into two groups and hold a mock public hearing, as suggested on page 66.

5. Follow the directions on page 62 to create electricity montages. Use the completed art projects to decorate the room for the "Electricity Fair" (page 68).

Electricity – A Household Word

At Home Activity

- Make a list of electrical appliances and other items that require electricity in your home. In the spaces below, list these items in the appropriate room.

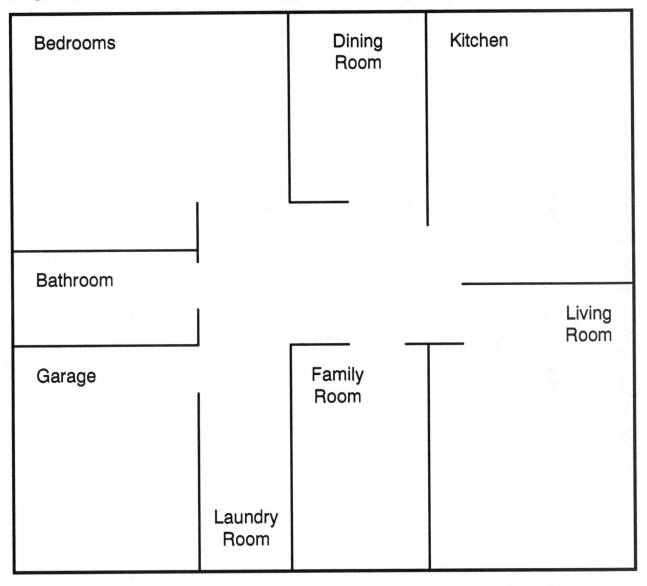

- Draw a blue star next to items that are used daily. Draw a red square next to items that are used several times a week. Draw a green circle next to items that are used a few times a month. Draw an orange triangle next to items used a few times a year.

- Count the number of items that have stars, squares, circles, and triangles drawn next to them. Use the information to complete the bar graph on page 20.

Electricity – A Household Word *(cont.)*

Directions: Fill in the following bar graph after you have completed the activity on page 19.

Using Electrical Items in the Home

Number of Times Used

30	
25	
20	
15	
10	
5	
0	

Daily | Several Times a Week | A Few Times a Month | A Few Times a Year

Appliance Usage

Energy Facts

Directions: Learn some interesting facts about energy as you solve the problems below. Then write the letters from the box on the sentence blanks, matching the letters with the corresponding answers below the blanks.

A	C	D	E	G	H
37 x 12 = _____	659 + 13 = _____	720 ÷ 16 = _____	316 – 105 = _____	67 + 39 = _____	374 ÷ 22 = _____
I	**K**	**L**	**M**	**N**	**O**
823 – 78 = _____	16 x 15 = _____	361 + 19 = _____	957 ÷ 33 = _____	500 – 135 = _____	17 x 9 = _____
R	**S**	**T**	**U**	**W**	**Y**
369 + 72 = _____	216 ÷ 8 = _____	999 – 955 = _____	62 x 4 = _____	416 + 41 = _____	488 ÷ 4 = _____

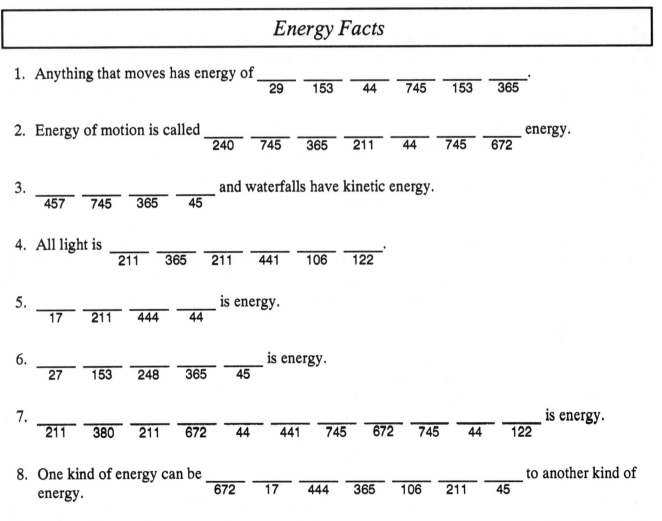

Energy Facts

1. Anything that moves has energy of ____ ____ ____ ____ ____ ____ .
   29   153   44   745   153   365

2. Energy of motion is called ____ ____ ____ ____ ____ ____ ____ energy.
   240   745   365   211   44   745   672

3. ____ ____ ____ ____ and waterfalls have kinetic energy.
   457   745   365   45

4. All light is ____ ____ ____ ____ ____ ____ .
   211   365   211   441   106   122

5. ____ ____ ____ ____ is energy.
   17   211   444   44

6. ____ ____ ____ ____ ____ is energy.
   27   153   248   365   45

7. ____ ____ ____ ____ ____ ____ ____ ____ ____ ____ ____ is energy.
   211   380   211   672   44   441   745   672   745   44   122

8. One kind of energy can be ____ ____ ____ ____ ____ ____ ____ to another kind of energy.
   672   17   444   365   106   211   45

Magic and Magnetism

Time for a Little Levity!

Have you ever seen a magician make an object or person "float"? He or she is performing levitation. You, too, can be a magician by using magnets to make things seem to float in the air, or levitate.

Try the following magic on your friends.

Materials: paper clips, strong horseshoe magnet, cotton thread, sheet of paper, tape

Directions: Begin by tying one end of a length of cotton thread to a paper clip. Tape the opposite end of the thread to a tabletop. (It may be necessary to lengthen or shorten the thread in order to levitate the paper clip more easily.) Place the magnet near the paper clip so that the clip is drawn to the magnet but not touching it. This may take a little practice at first. Carefully levitate the paper clip by moving the magnet away from the table. To show that the magnet and paper clip are not touching each other, pass a sheet of paper between them.

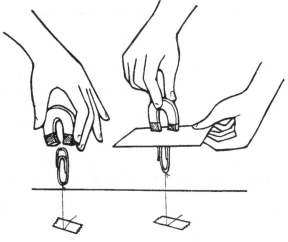

The levitation magic you have just done with magnets has been put to use to create modern, high-speed trains in Germany and Japan. This form of transportation will most likely expand in the coming years. Read about this exciting means of travel at the following Web sites.

Internet Extender

Magnetic Levitation Train

http://www.mvp.de/

Activity Summary: Visit this Web site and select the English version to see photos and read the description of the exciting new type of transportation which uses magnetic levitation to operate a high-speed train system developed in Germany. Click on "Fotos" to see more pictures of this new train. The information about these photos is in German only.

The Maglev System

http://www.rtri.or.jp/rd/maglev/html/english/maglev_principle_E.html

Activity Summary: Find out about the history of the Maglev (Magnetic Levitation) system. Click on "Principle of Maglev" to see illustrations that show how magnets are used to run the trains.

22

All Steamed Up!

The steam turbine can produce a great deal of power to run machinery. It can be used to drive electric generators in huge power stations and to run ocean liners.

Directions: Identify the parts of the steam turbine by writing the terms from the word bank on the lines of the diagram. On another sheet of paper answer the questions below the diagram.

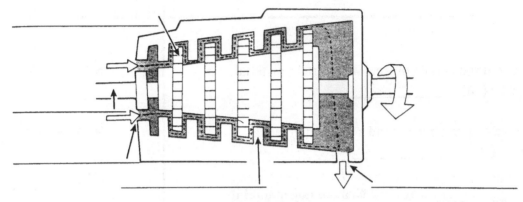

Word Bank

- turbine wheels
- stationary blades
- shaft
- steam flow
- steam exhaust

1. How is steam produced in most power plants?
2. What happens when steam builds up in the boilers?
3. What is at the other end of the turbine shaft?
4. What are some examples of machines or other devices powered by steam turbines

---

Internet Extender

Visit the following Web sites to learn about Hoover Dam, a hydroelectric plant which uses turbines. Discuss what students have learned after they read about this dam.

Hoover Dam

http://www.hooverdam.com/History/index.htm

Activity Summary: Have students follow links from this homepage to learn about the history of this dam through short essays and personal experiences, how it works, and the dramatic testing of the Jetflow Gate in 1998.

Learn about other ways of producing power from the following Web site.

Producing Electricity

http://www.photovault.com/Link/Technology/Power_Hydroelectric.html

Activity Summary: This Web site has many photographs showing power plants which use a variety of sources, including solar, wind, hydroelectric, and fossil fuels.

Electricity Match-Up

Directions: Complete each sentence in column A by writing the letter of the correct term from column B in the space provided at the end of the corresponding sentence.

Column A	Column B
1. When you rub certain objects with certain material, you get a (an) _____.	A. conductors
2. The area of attraction around a charged object is called a (an) _____.	B. electric charge
3. _____ stays in a charged object until it disappears into the air, the ground, or some other object.	C. hydroelectric
4. Materials that move electricity through them instead of becoming charged are called _____.	D. magnetic field
5. Moving electricity is called _____.	E. electric field
6. Materials that can pick up or attract metals such as iron or steel are called _____.	F. generator
7. The area around the magnet that pulls on metals is called its _____.	G. static electricity
8. The arrangement of moving magnets and wire coil is called a (an) _____.	H. magnets
9. The arrangement of a shaft and blades on the other end of a generator is called a (an) _____.	I. turbine
10. A _____ power plant uses flowing water to produce electricity.	J. current electricity

Get a Charge Out of It!

Have you ever dragged your shoes across a rug and put your finger close to a metal object? What happens? The shock that you received was caused by static electricity. Static electricity is produced by friction, or the rubbing of two different materials together. This type of electricity does not move; it is stationary, or static.

Have some fun with the effects of static electricity with the following activities.

The Main Attraction

Materials: balloon; sink with running water; clean, dry cloth

Directions: Allow an unbroken stream of water to run from the tap. Inflate a balloon and tie the neck in a knot. Rub the balloon with a cloth several times to "charge" it. Then, hold it near the stream of water. Observe what happens. (The flow of water bends toward the balloon.)

Explanation: As you rub the balloon with the cloth, a charge of static electricity is created. An electrical force strong enough to attract the water surrounds the balloon.

Extension: Follow the directions above once again. After the stream of water bends, touch the balloon to the water. Pull it away from the stream and place it near the water again. What do you observe? What do you think caused this reaction? Discuss your ideas with classmates.

Balloon Keep-Away

Materials: 2 inflated balloons; piece of string (about 4 feet/1.2 meters); piece of paper; wool fabric

Directions: Tie one end of the string to the neck of each balloon. Create static electricity by rubbing the balloons against the wool fabric. Hold the string at its midpoint and hang the balloons as shown. What happens? Place a piece of paper between the balloons and observe what happens. Now remove the paper. What happens?

Explanation: When the "electrified" balloons hang next to each other, they separate because a negative charge forces them to repel each other.

When the paper is introduced, the balloons "give" a positive charge to the paper and are attracted to it, causing the balloons to come closer together. Once the paper is removed, the negative charges of the balloons force them to separate once again.

Get a Charge Out of It!

Make a Static Electricity Detector

Materials: sewing needle, pattern (below) reproduced on index paper, scissors, 5-ounce (150 mL) paper cup, inflated balloon, wool fabric

Directions: Cut out the pattern ("arm" of the detector). Turn the paper cup upside down on a tabletop. Insert a sewing needle vertically into the detector arm at the mark. Push the needle through the pattern and the center of the paper cup as shown. Allow enough of the needle to protrude at the bottom of the pattern so that the detector arm can swing freely. Rub the balloon with a piece of wool fabric and hold it near the arm of the detector. What happens? (**Note:** You may test other objects for the presence of static electricity. Simply rub each object with wool and place it near the detector.)

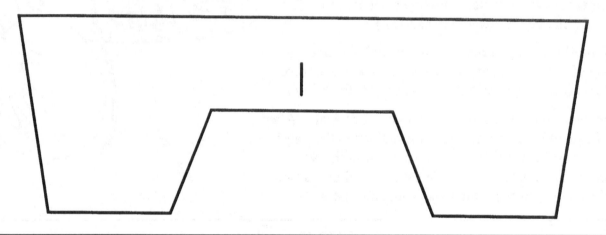

Internet Extender

Static Electric Generator

http://www.alaska.net/~natnkell/staticgen.htm

Activity Summary: This Web site is for teachers and provides ideas for making a static electricity generator which uses simple material to give off a visible spark.

Dramatic Static

http://www.exploratorium.edu/science_explorer/

Activity Summary: At this Web site, scan down to the Dramatic Static section and click on "Super Sparker." Follow the instructions to make this safe, fun static electric experiment with simple materials. Return to the home page and click on "Remote Control Roller" to find how you can use a balloon to roll an empty aluminum can around. Information on what makes these experiments work is provided.

Venn Diagram

As more electricity is produced, valuable resources, such as coal, oil, and gas are used in an effort to keep up with the demand. Alternate energy sources (solar, geothermal, nuclear, wind, and tides) are being considered as replacements. Research to find out more about present and future sources of energy. Choose two sources. Write their similarities and differences in the appropriate areas of the Venn diagram below.

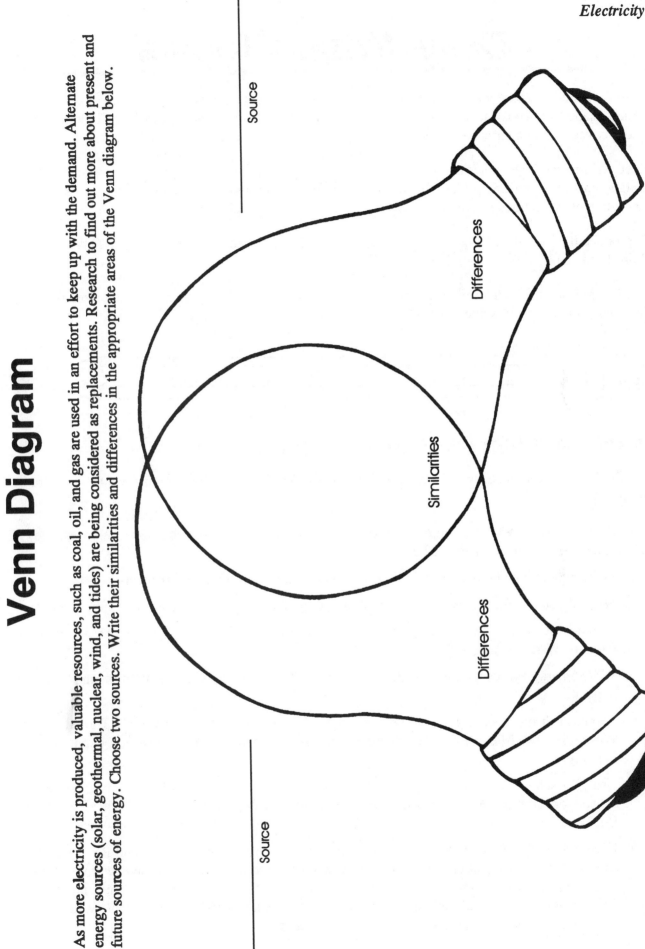

Source

Differences

Similarities

Differences

Source

Daily Writing Topics

Have each student create his or her own writing folder. Students may use file folders, pocket folders, or folders made from construction paper. Have students cut out the pattern on page 32 and glue it on a folder cover. As an alternative, students can design a cover for the front of their folders.

Keep writing activities, notes and brainstorming ideas, research information, and other related assignments in the writing folders for storage and reference throughout the unit. You may also wish to have students keep track of any theme-related handouts you may give them.

Reproduce the "Word Bank" on page 35 as a handy resource for each student. Have students keep the Word Banks in their writing folders.

Encourage students to choose ideas from the writing topics below. Have them write on a regular basis and share some of their written ideas.

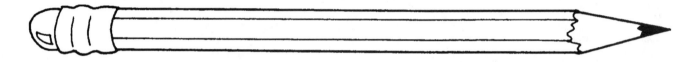

Inventors and Their Inventions

Use the information on pages 9–13 and other resources to write about the famous inventors you studied in this unit.

1. Pretend you are a young Thomas Edison. Write a paragraph on how you feel when everyone calls you "stupid, "dunce," and "addled."

2. Write a paragraph on the results of one of Young Tom's "mischief" experiments.

3. Pretend you are Tom as a telegraph operator. Write a letter to your family explaining your job.

4. Pretend you are a newspaper reporter. Write an interview with Edison, Latimer, Morse, Bell, or Faraday. Write the pros and cons of one of Edison's inventions.

5. Write a paragraph explaining this Edison quote: "Genius is one percent inspiration and 99 percent perspiration."

6. Thomas Edison was intrigued by the work of Michael Faraday. Imagine you are Thomas Edison. Write a letter to Michael Faraday. Include some questions you, as Edison, would like to ask Mr. Faraday.

7. Use your school or public library to locate additional information about Bell, Morse, Faraday, Edison, or Latimer. Write a magazine or journal article titled "Without Them, Where Would We Be?" and include your research and ideas about how far-reaching their inventions were.

8. Lewis Howard Latimer's life spanned the time from slavery to the Civil War and Reconstruction and on into the last quarter of the nineteenth century to the first quarter of the twentieth century. During these times a number of social and technological changes took place in the United States and throughout the world. Make a list of several technological changes that occurred during Latimer's lifetime. Choose one change and write about it.

Daily Writing Topics *(cont.)*

Inventors and Their Inventions *(cont.)*

9. Lewis Howard Latimer worked with Alexander Graham Bell on the design for the device we now know as the telephone. Bell believed that his invention would make it possible for deaf people to hear speech. Do some reading about Alexander Graham Bell to find out why he was interested in helping the deaf. Write about it in your journal.

10. Thomas Edison was convinced that a direct current was better than an alternating current. Latimer and other electricians felt that alternating current was the better choice. Find out the difference between alternating current and direct current. Based on what you discover, take a position on which type of current is more efficient. Write an argument to support that position.

Electricity

1. Describe what it is like at your home when the power goes out.

2. Bring an electric bill from home. Write an explanation of the bill.

3. Lightning is almost impossible to control. If you had a power to control it, what would you do? Write an article on how you would harness lightning and to what uses you would apply its energy.

4. Have you had a memorable moment with static electricity? Write a paragraph explaining what happened.

5. Explain the need for a magnetic field in generating electricity.

6. Discover the type of energy source your power company uses to generate electricity. Write an article about it.

7. Write an editorial on the negative aspects of burning fossil fuels.

8. Write an editorial on the energy crisis.

9. Write an editorial on the need for alternate energy.

10. Write an editorial in favor of (or opposed to) nuclear energy.

11. Write an article describing which alternate energy ideas would work in your area. Use supporting evidence.

12. Write an article about what you can do to save energy.

13. Interview someone who lived for an extended period of time without electricity.

Create Your Own Books

Have students make books using various suggestions throughout the unit. You can use the suggestions in the "Daily Writing Topics" (pages 28-29) or ideas introduced by students. Students writing books in groups or individually may consider an elaborate format, such as the following, or a much simpler one.

Parts of a Book

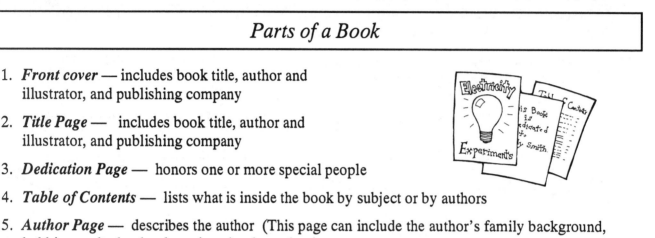

1. *Front cover* — includes book title, author and illustrator, and publishing company

2. *Title Page* — includes book title, author and illustrator, and publishing company

3. *Dedication Page* — honors one or more special people

4. *Table of Contents* — lists what is inside the book by subject or by authors

5. *Author Page* — describes the author (This page can include the author's family background, hobbies, and other books written by the author.)

6. *Back Cover* — may include an illustration and book reviews from magazines, book clubs, newspapers, etc.

Several methods for making books are introduced below and on page 31. Select one appropriate to the book topic and purpose.

Big Books

Ready-made, blank Big Books are available at educational supply stores. If you wish to make your own, follow the directions below.

Materials: tagboard or heavy paper; metal rings; hole reinforcers; crayons; colored pencils or markers; scissors; glue

Directions

- Punch three holes on the left hand side of each sheet of tagboard or heavy paper. Cover the front and back of each hole with reinforcers.

- Have students write the text, adding illustrations where appropriate, on each page or on paper strips which can be glued to the pages.

- When all pages are completed, have students put the pages in order and make a front and back cover for the Big Book. Connect all pages with metal rings.

- Have students share their Big Books with other students or classes. Display Big Books on a large table along with projects on electricity.

Create Your Own Books *(cont.)*

Shape Books

Materials: construction paper, tagboard, or heavy paper; crayons, colored pencils or markers; pencil; scissors; stapler

Directions

- Reproduce enough copies of the shape book pattern on page 32 to use as book pages.

- Provide each student, or group of students, with a copy of the pattern for the cover. You may wish to reproduce covers on a different color of paper. If available, use index paper to create a heavier book cover.

- Have students write the text and on each page. Encourage them to include illustrations. Arrange the finished pages in order and staple them together along one edge.

Wheel Books

Materials: construction paper or tagboard; scissors; crayons or colored pencils; brad fasteners; pencil

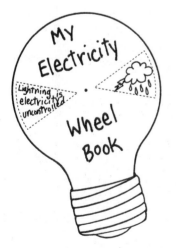

Directions

- Make copies of the patterns on pages 33-34.

- Have students cut out the wheel pattern, the light bulb, and the dashed "windows" on the light bulb.

- Help students attach the center of the wheel behind the bulb with a brad fastener. Direct students to color their light bulbs.

- Next, have students draw a picture relating information about electricity in the wheel section on the right side of the light bulb. In the wheel section on the left side of the light bulb, have students write a sentence or a word describing the picture.

To complete the wheel book, have students turn their wheels to the next blank section, draw another picture and repeat the procedure described above until all wheel sections have been filled in.

Writing

Shape Book Pattern

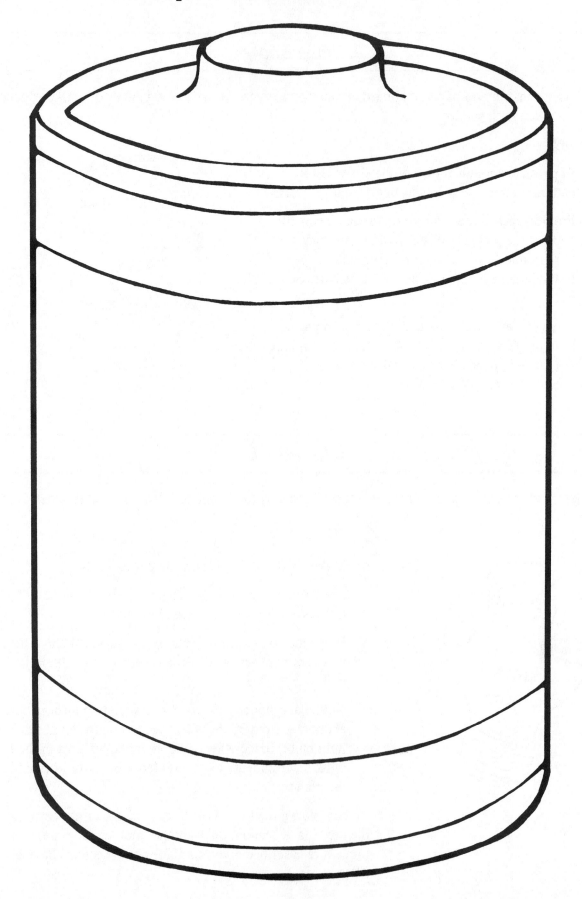

32

Wheel Book Pattern

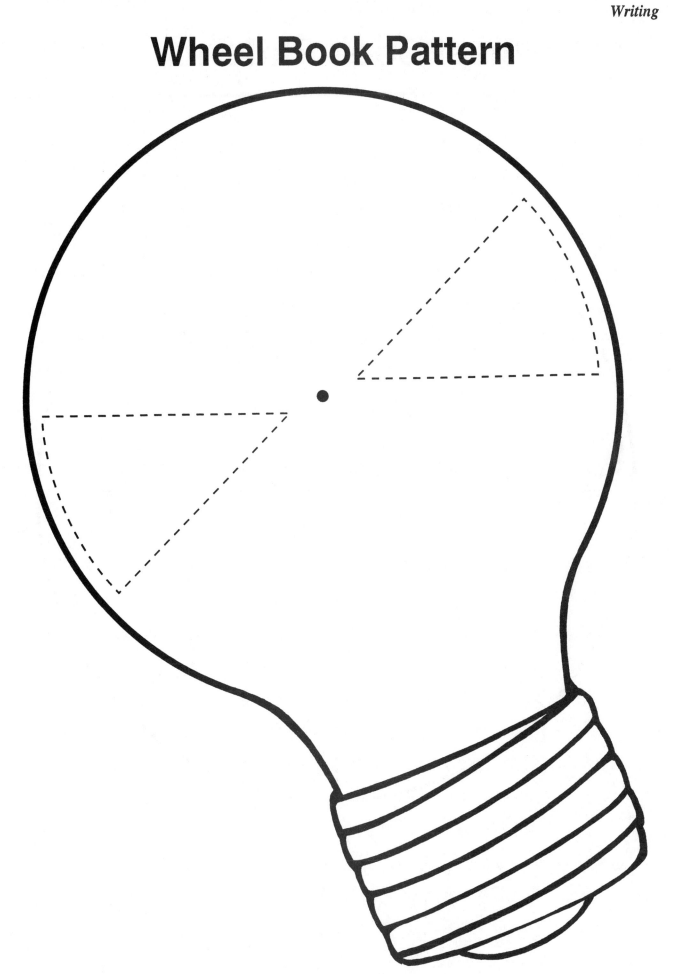

Wheel Book Pattern *(cont.)*

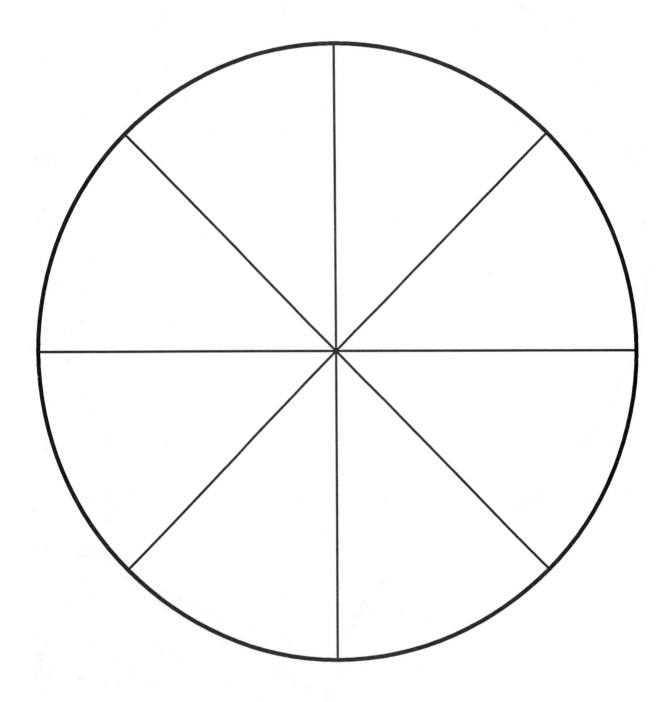

Word Bank

Edison's Inventions and Contributions to Inventions

diplex telegraph	motion picture	stockticker
electric light bulb	phonograph	telegraph
goldticker	quadruplex telegraph	telephone

Inventors and Scientists

Thomas Alva Edison	Andre Ampere	John Kruesi
Samuel F.B. Morse	Michael Faraday	John Ott
Alexander Graham Bell	Alessandro Volta	George D. Little
Sigmund Bergmann	Charles Batchelor	Henry Ford
Sir Humphrey Davy	William A. Hart	William Murdock
Hans Christian Oersted	Charles F. Brush	Sir William Crokes
D. McFarlan Moore	Arturo Malignani	Benjamin Franklin
George Westinghouse	G.S. Ohm	

Electrical Terms

alternating current	filament	nonconductor
ampere	fuse	nucleus
atom	fossil fuel	receptacle
chain reaction	fuel cell	solar cell
circuit	generating station	static electricity
circuit breaker	generator	transmission line
conductor	geothermal generating station	turbine
connecting cord	hydroelectric	uranium
current electricity	insulators	magnetic field
direct current	kilowatt	proton
electromagnet	lines of force	transformer
electron	magnet	volt
element	neutron	watt

Crossword Puzzle

To acquaint you with names and terms that will be used throughout this thematic unit, complete the puzzle below using the words from the word list at the bottom of the page.

Clues

Across

1. inventor of the telephone
6. a measure of large quantities of electric power
9. the center of an atom
10. an engine; revolving motor
11. nuclear energy
14. a tall, steel tower that carries electrical wires
15. one of the parts of the atom
16. materials that are bad conductors

Down

2. inventor of the light bulb
3. a thin wire inside an electric bulb
4. iron or steel that has the power to attract other iron or steel
5. a tiny particle of matter
7. inventor of the telegraph
8. moving magnet and wire coil used in making electricity
12. a substance in which electricity flows easily
13. device used for transmitting messages by wire

Word List			
atom	magnet	Bell	Morse
conductor	nucleus	Edison	proton
filament	pylon	generator	radioactivity
insulators	telegraph	kilowatt	turbine

Get the Message

The telegraph was one of the greatest inventions of the mid-nineteenth century. It was invented in 1838 by Samuel F. B. Morse. He devised a code using a series of "dots" and "dashes" that represented the letters of the alphabet. Messages were tapped out on a telegraph key that made clicking sounds. A dot would be a short click, and a dash would be a longer click. Messages would be carried electrically to another key where a second operator would translate the message back into English and write it down on paper.

Directions: Use the following code to change the words below into Morse code. (You may find slight variation from other codes.) You may also wish to use the Morse code to send messages back and forth to friends.

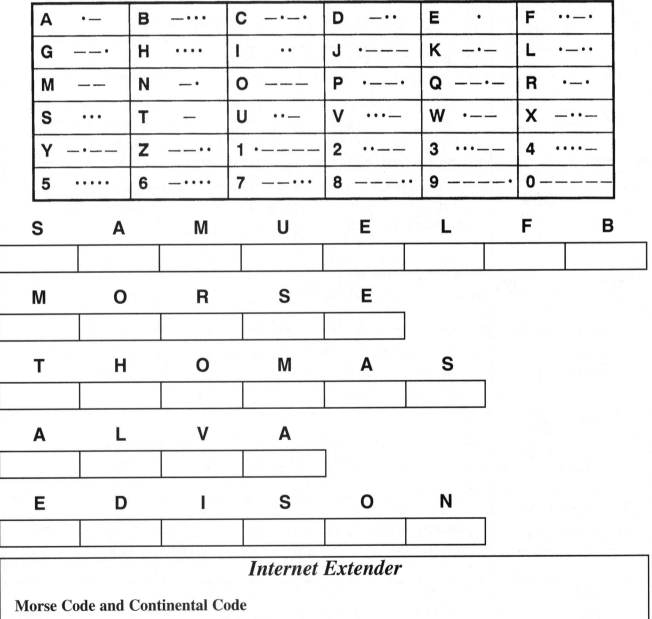

Internet Extender

Morse Code and Continental Code

http://www.chss.montclair.edu/~pererat/percode.html

Activity Summary: Discover the Continental Code, introduced in England in the 1800s, as shown at this Web site. Create new messages using this code for the names on this page.

Electricity Facts

Directions: Solve each problem below. Then write the answer in the blank to find out some interesting facts about electricity.

1.	$\begin{array}{r} 932 \\ + 963 \\ \hline \end{array}$	The world's first hydroelectric A.C. generating plant began operation at Niagara Falls, New York, in _____.
2.	$\begin{array}{r} 1288 \\ + 687 \\ \hline \end{array}$	One of the nation's largest solar heating and cooling systems has been in operation since _____ at the George A. Towns Elementary School in Atlanta, Georgia.
3.	$100 \times 20 =$ ___	"Solar One", a solar power test plant near Barstow, California, has _____ mirrors which reflect solar heat to a central receiver, producing steam to operate an electricity-producing turbine.
4.	$\begin{array}{r} 479 \\ - 359 \\ \hline \end{array}$	To make electricity, we must push electrons through a circuit. It takes pressure. We measure electric pressure in volts. The electric pressure in your home is probably _____ volts.
5.	$101 -$ ___ $= 86$	Ampere measures how much electricity is being pushed through a circuit. Some wires can safely carry _____ amperes.
6.	$100 \div 5 =$ ___	Watts measure the amount of electric power we are using to run machines, light a lamp, etc. A small light bulb uses a little electric power, maybe it'll be a _____ watt bulb.
7.	$\begin{array}{r} 250 \\ \times 4 \\ \hline \end{array}$	Kilowatt is a large amount of electric power. One kilowatt = _____ watts. Big electric kitchen stoves can use 10 kilowatts of power.
8.	$\begin{array}{r} 258 \\ + 179 \\ \hline \end{array}$	In western Kentucky, there is a large fuel-powered steam generating plant. There are three _____ foot high cooling towers.
9.	$51 +$ ___ $= 66$	If a wire in your circuit carries as much as _____ amperes of electricity, then you need a fuse to protect your circuit of amperes.

Be a Meter Reader

An electric meter measures how much electric power is being used at the location to which it is connected. The dials are like clock faces, with one hand on each face. They indicate the minutes and hours you are using electricity. They measure in kilowatt-hours.

Directions: Look at the following meters. All of these meters were read on the first of each month. Use the sample provided to determine the meter readings at Ted's and Mary's houses. Then answer the "Kilowatt Questions" at the bottom of the page.

Sample House

This meter reads
2,795 kilowatt-hours.

Ted's House
May
This meter reads
_____ kilowatt-hours.

Ted's House
June
This meter reads
_____ kilowatt-hours.

Mary's House
May
This meter reads
_____ kilowatt-hours.

Mary's House
June
This meter reads
_____ kilowatt-hours.

Kilowatt Questions

1. How many kilowatt-hours were used in Ted's house in May? _____

2. How many kilowatt-hours were used in Mary's house in May? _____

3. Which household used the most electricity during May? _____

4. How many more kilowatt-hours were used in Mary's house than in Ted's house? _____

What's the Charge?

A household is charged on its monthly electric bill for each kilowatt-hour (kwh) of electricity used, based on the meter reading and the rate (cost) for the kilowatt-hour. (A kilowatt represents 1000 watts of electrical energy.)

Directions: Use the information on the chart below to complete the line graph on this page. The completed graph represents the amount of kilowatt-hours of electricity used each month. Then, use the data from the graph and chart to answer the "Kilowatt Questions" and "Calculator Corner" problems at the bottom of the page.

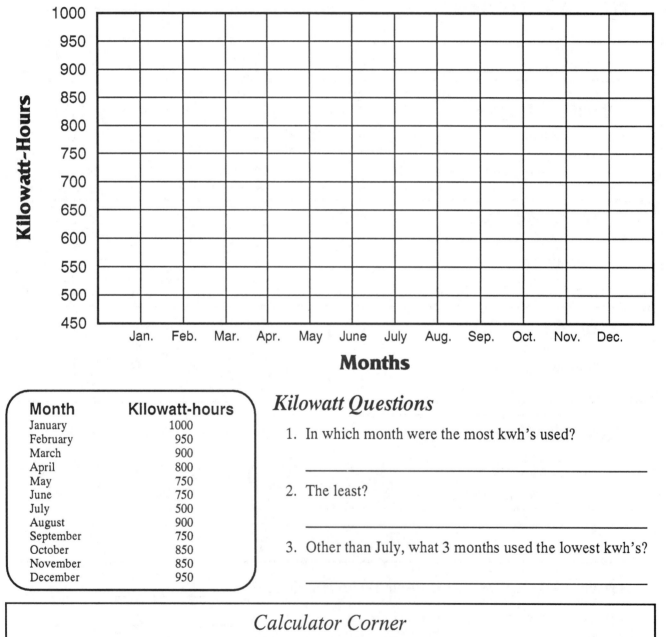

Month	Kilowatt-hours
January	1000
February	950
March	900
April	800
May	750
June	750
July	500
August	900
September	750
October	850
November	850
December	950

Kilowatt Questions

1. In which month were the most kwh's used?

   _____

2. The least?

   _____

3. Other than July, what 3 months used the lowest kwh's?

   _____

Calculator Corner

Use a calculator to determine the charge for each month based on this formula: 1 kwh = $.005. Write your answers on the back of this page.

How Many Amperes?

How much electricity does each of these household appliances use? To find the answer, you will need to know about electrical units of measure called amperes, watts, and volts and how to use them to find out the rate at which electricity flows (amperes) through the electric current that "runs" the appliance.

- An *ampere* (abbreviated, amp.) is an electrical unit of measure. It indicates the rate of flow of an electric current.

- A *watt* measures electrical power. It indicates how fast electrical energy is being used.

- A *volt* is a unit of electrical pressure. It measures the force pushing electrons through a conductor.

Directions: Find the amperes of electricity for each of the following appliances. The number representing watts and volts for each appliance is provided in the chart. To obtain amperes, divide watts by volts. The first item is done for you. Write the solution to each problem in the space provided. Round off the amperes to the nearest whole number. Use a calculator if necessary. Then, answer the questions at the bottom of the page.

(Equation: Watts ÷ Volts = Amperes)

Item	Watts	Volts	Amperes
stereo	300	110	2.7 (round to 3 Amperes)
air conditioner	1350	110	
blender	250	110	
electric can opener	150	110	
coffee maker	600	110	
dryer	6000	110	
freezer	350	110	
iron	1000	110	
floor lamp	300	110	
mixer	150	110	
electric range	12,000	110	
refrigerator	250	110	
television	300	110	
toaster	110	110	
vacuum cleaner	400	110	
washing machine	350	110	

Questions

1. Which items can not be run on a 15 ampere circuit? _____

2. Which two items use the most amperes? What feature do they have in common?

_____

Overload

When a wire carries more electricity than it should, the wire is overloaded. This creates a possible fire hazard because the wires can become overheated by carrying more electrons (electric current) than they were designed to safely transport. To protect wires from overheating, a fuse or circuit breaker is installed. The fuse or circuit breaker is connected to the electric circuit. If the current passing through one of these safety devices is too much for the circuit to handle, the fuse or circuit breaker acts like an emergency switch, stopping the flow of electricity.

Directions: Find out how safe each of the following circuits is. Use the information from the chart on page 41 to decide if a circuit is overloaded. Assume your circuits have fuses capable of carrying no more than 15 amps. Determine the total amount of amperes being used in each circuit if all the appliances are running at the same time. Then, answer the questions at the bottom of the page.

Circuit 1
Total _____

refrigerator	coffee maker	can opener
_____ *amps*	_____ *amps*	_____ *amps*
blender	toaster	air conditioner
_____ *amps*	_____ *amps*	_____ *amps*

Circuit 2
Total _____

floor lamp	television
_____ *amps*	_____ *amps*
floor lamp	stereo
_____ *amps*	_____ *amps*

Circuit 3
Total _____

freezer	refrigerator	television
_____ *amps*	_____ *amps*	_____ *amps*
mixer	can opener	
_____ *amps*	_____ *amps*	

Circuit 4
Total _____

washing machine	television
_____ *amps*	_____ *amps*
iron	air conditioner
_____ *amps*	_____ *amps*

Questions

1. Which two circuits are safe? _____ and _____

2. How could you change Circuit 1 to make it safe? _____

3. In which circuit could you safely run a vacuum cleaner? _____

Electrician's Math

Calculator Corner

Directions: Use a calculator and the equations on this page to complete the chart below. Then, answer the questions at the bottom of the page.

Apply the following abbreviations to the formulas in the box below the chart: *watts = W; kilowatts = KW; amperes = AMPS; volts = 110; 1kw = 1,000W*

Item	Watts/W	Kilowatts/KW (Round to the nearest tenth)	Amperes/AMPS (Round to the nearest tenth)
1. central air conditioner		5	
2. dishwasher			16.4
3. food warmer	500		
4. fryer			12
5. furnace		.3	
6. garbage disposer	900		
7. grill		1.3	
8. hot water heater	2500		
9. sun lamp			2.5

Formulas

AMPS x 110 = W   W÷ 1,000 = KW   AMPS x .110 = KW

KWx 1,000 = W   W÷ 110 = AMPS   KW÷ .110 = AMPS

Questions

1. How many items can be used on a 15 ampere circuit? _____

2. What items are they? _____

Shedding Light on the Subject

Do you have an electrical switch in your house that allows you to dim a light? This type of switch controls the brightness or dimness of a light source with a device called a rheostat. To find out how a rheostat works, try the following activity.

Materials: clear (transparent) tape; 10" (25 cm) length of thin; copper wire; unused length of lead from a mechanical pencil; flashlight bulb; flashlight battery

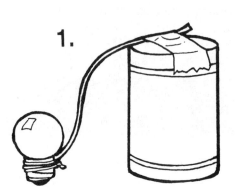

Directions

1. Use tape to attach one end of the copper wire to the top of the battery. Connect the other end of the wire to the light bulb by twisting the wire several times around the metal base of the bulb.

2. Put the pencil lead on a smooth, flat surface. Gently place the bottom of the battery on one end of the lead and rest the bottom of the light bulb on the lead, close to the battery. Observe the light from the bulb.

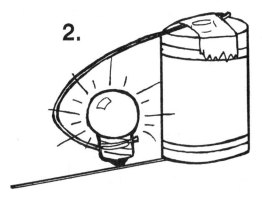

3. Slide the light bulb toward the far end of the pencil lead. Observe the light from the bulb. Is the bulb brighter or dimmer than it was when you placed it close to the battery?

Explanation: The pencil lead makes a good rheostat because it allows you to adjust the brightness or dimness of the light by controlling the electric current flowing through it. When the light bulb is close to the battery, the current is stronger. The bulb dims as it is moved away from the battery.

Thinking Like a Scientist

A scientist asks many questions and performs experiments to discover the answers. Thomas Alva Edison was such a scientist. He learned by reading many books that interested him. As a young man, Thomas Edison performed many of the experiments introduced in these books and was motivated to begin scientific experiments of his own.

Thomas Edison said, "Be sure a thing is needed or wanted, then go ahead." Like other scientists, Thomas Edison found the answers to his questions through experimentation. On other occasions, his questions may have lead him to ask more questions and try new experiments to find the answers.

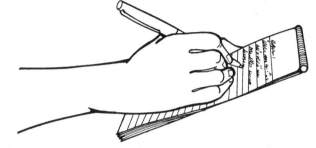

How Does a Scientist Think?

- A scientist often makes an **OBSERVATION** that leads him or her to ask a **QUESTION**. In order to solve a problem or answer a question, a scientist does research by investigating and gathering facts about a subject.

- Then the scientist develops an **HYPOTHESIS**, which is a prediction of what he/she thinks will happen.

- Next, the scientist develops a test plan, or **PROCEDURE**, to determine the materials he or she will need. A scientist tests the hypothesis by using the procedure in the form of an experiment. An experiment is a way to test what happens to something.

- The scientist collects data, or information, by observing, measuring, and carefully recording the **RESULTS** or outcome of the experiment.

- The scientist now examines the data and comes to a **CONCLUSION**, or final decision about what happened. It is just as important to record failures as well as successes. Finally, a scientist writes a report about the findings (results), so that others can learn from the experiments. Scientists follow these procedures (step-by-step way of doing things), for each experiment they do.

This method of solving a problem by asking a question raised from an observation, making a prediction (hypothesis) about what will happen, following a planned procedure to test the hypothesis, and using the results to come to a conclusion about what the results mean, is called the **SCIENTIFIC METHOD**.

The scientific method is a step-by-step way of thinking through a problem. You can use this "thinking process" to solve problems in areas other than science by first considering the problem and what you think the solution should be. Then, make a step-by-step plan of how you will solve the problem. Carry out the plan. Finally, take a close look at your solution to see whether or not it answers the question or solves your problem.

You, too, can think like a scientist. Choose several of the science activities in this unit. For each activity you select, use the steps of the scientific method to complete the form on page 46.

Experiment Form

Scientist _____

Title of Activity _____

Observation: What caused you to ask the question?

_____

_____

_____

Question: What do you want to find out?

_____

_____

_____

Hypothesis: What do you think you will find out?

_____

_____

_____

Procedure: How will you find out? (List step by step. Use the back of this page if necessary.)

1. _____
2. _____
3. _____
4. _____

Result(s):   What actually happened?

_____

_____

_____

Conclusion(s):   What did you learn?

_____

_____

_____

Keep the Motor Running!

Electricity can be used to produce power and motion. It can run motors. A motor uses electricity to produce magnetism. The motor changes electrical energy to mechanical energy. Find out how motors work by building this simple motor.

Materials: pencil; solid copper or aluminum wire; flashlight battery; cardboard; horseshoe magnet; small copper wire, cut into 2 pieces, each about 2 feet (.6 meters); scissors; pliers

Directions

1. Cut out a 24" x 6" (61 cm x 15 cm) piece of cardboard. Fold the cardboard into thirds (lengthwise) so that each section is 8" (20 cm) long.

2. With the cardboard ends facing up on a flat surface, poke a pencil near the top of each end, as shown.

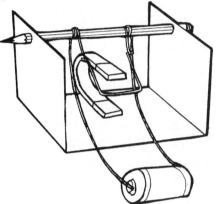

3. Bend a short piece of copper or aluminum wire to form a "U" shape. Turn the ends of the wire out about ¼" (.6 cm). (Use pliers where necessary.)

4. Wrap the end of one of the small pieces of copper wire to a bent end of the "U" shaped wire. Make sure the wire is wrapped tightly. Do the same with the other small piece of copper wire.

5. Wrap each of the small copper wire pieces around the pencil, as shown, suspending the copper wire "U" from the pencil.

6. Place the horseshoe magnet on its side, allowing the copper "U" to swing freely between the magnet's poles.

7. Connect the loose end of each small copper wire to one of the ends of a flashlight battery. The copper "U" will swing toward or away from the magnet. Switch each wire connection to the opposite end of the battery and observe what happens. The copper "U" should now swing in the opposite direction.

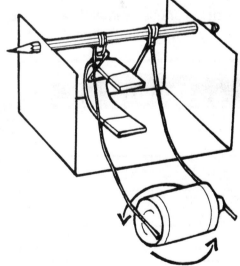

Explanation: When the wires are connected to the battery, a circuit is completed and current flows through the copper "U", creating an electromagnet. When the wires are connected to the battery in one way, the current flows in a specific direction, causing the magnet to attract the copper "U." When the connection is reversed, current flows in the opposite direction, and the magnet repels (pushes away) the copper "U." If this process is speeded up, as it is in a motor, it forces the magnet to attract and repel so rapidly that a continuous motion results and you can "keep the motor running."

Material Conductors

A conductor is a material which allows electricity to flow easily through it. Follow the directions below to make an electrical circuit and test various materials to discover which ones conduct electricity.

Materials: 1.5-volt ("C") battery; 1.5-volt flashlight bulb; 12" (30 cm) length of flexible, insulated copper wire; wire strippers; tape; assortment of materials, including rock, cloth, wood, metals, glass, paper, etc.

Directions

1. Have an adult strip away about 2" (5 cm) of insulation from the ends of the copper wire. Twist one end of the wire tightly around the metal part of the light bulb. Securely tape the other stripped end of the wire to the bottom of the battery. Touch the contact point at the bottom of the bulb to the terminal at the top of the battery. What happens? When the bulb lights, an electrical circuit has been completed.

2. Test the collected materials and observe which ones light the bulb (indicating that they allow electricity to flow through them). One by one, place the different materials between the light bulb and the battery terminal, as shown. Make certain the material touches both the terminal and the contact at the bottom of the bulb. The bulb should light up whenever the material is a conductor. It does not light when the material is a non-conductor.

3. Write your observations below. Use the back of this page if necessary. Then, fill out the "Experiment Form" on page 46.

Material	(Check one.)	
	Conductor	**Nonconductor**

Electromagnets

As an electric current passes through a wire, a magnetic field forms around the wire. Electromagnets are objects in which magnetism is induced by electricity. They are temporary magnets because they lose their magnetic properties when the flow of electricity is discontinued.

Follow the directions and diagrams below to make and use three simple electromagnets. You will need the following materials: a 1.5-volt ("C") battery; a large iron nail; tape; a 20" (50 cm) piece of thin, insulated copper wire; wire strippers; paper clips; a pencil; and a craft knife. After testing the electromagnets, complete the "Think About It" questions at the bottom of this page.

Electromagnet #1

An electric current flowing through a wire makes the wire magnetic. Strip the ends of the wire. Connect one end to the top of the battery. Connect the other wire end to the bottom of the battery. Try to pick up paper clips at the middle section of the wire. You should be able to pick up 1 or 2 clips.

Electromagnet #2

Coiling insulated wire strengthens an electromagnetic field. Wind the wire many times around a pencil. Be sure to wind the wire in the same direction. Allow about 4" (10 cm) of wire to protrude from each end of the pencil. Take out the pencil. Scrape off some of the insulation at one end of the coil. Try to pick up some paper clips with the uninsulated area of the coil. You should be able to pick up 3 or 4 clips.

Electromagnet #3

How does coiling a wire around a soft iron core affect the strength of the electromagnet? Coil the insulated wire tightly around an iron nail. With the ends of the wire, attach to the battery as before, pick up some paper clips with the coil-wrapped nail. How many clips were you able to pick up this time?

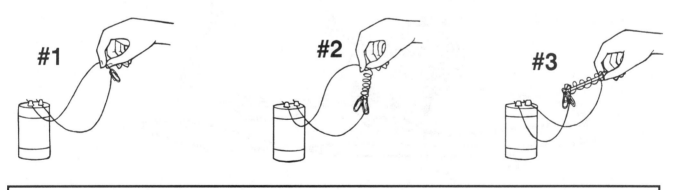

Think About It

- In which electromagnet experiment above were you able to pick up the most paper clips? Why do you think this happened?

- How can you make a stronger electromagnet? Write your idea on the back of this paper. Then experiment to test your idea. Use the form on page 46 to write your experiment and record the results. Share your experiment and conclusions with the class.

Homemade Batteries

You may have heard or read that Benjamin Franklin was the first person to discover that lightning is electricity. But did you know that he also invented the term "battery"? Ten years after Ben Franklin's death in 1800, Alessandro Volta invented the first battery. Follow the directions below to make your own battery. Then, try the extension activity with your homemade battery.

Materials: lemon; 12" (30 cm) piece of copper wire, cut into two equal pieces; nail; metal thumbtack; small flashlight bulb; scissors

Directions

1. Push the nail in near one end of the lemon. Push the thumbtack in near the other end of the lemon.

2. Twist one piece of the wire around the nail and the other piece around the thumbtack.

3. Touch the two free ends to the bumps on the bottom of the flashlight bulb. Observe what happens.

Extension: Using only one piece of copper wire, push the nail into one end of the lemon. Push the wire into the other end. Bend the wire towards the nail so they almost touch. Touch the earphone jack to the nail and copper wire simultaneously. Listen for the crackling static sounds.

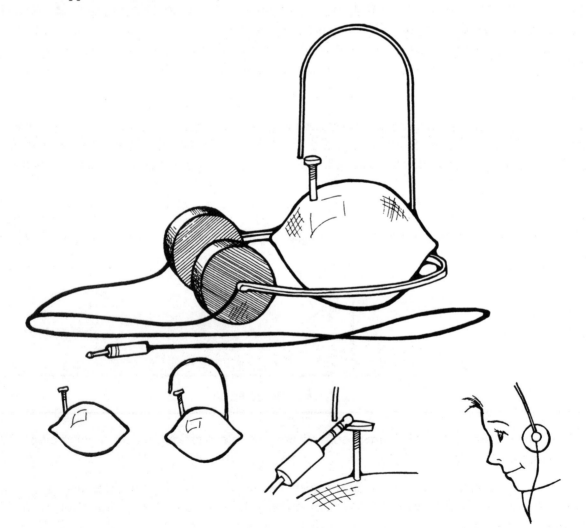

Build a Telegraph Set

Materials: 1.5-volt dry cell, about 10 feet (3 meters) thin insulated wire, 3" x .5" (8 cm x 1.3 cm) thin strip of metal, 2 small wood screws, demonstration light socket and bulb, 3" (8 cm) square block of wood, wire strippers, screwdriver

Directions

1. Cut the wire into three equal strips. Strip about 2" (5 cm) of insulation away from the wire ends.

2. Place a metal strip across the wood block and drive two screws into the block of wood as shown in the picture below. Be sure that one screw passes through the end of the metal strip, securing it to the block. Do not tighten the screws yet.

3. Attach the end of one wire to a terminal. Attach the end of a second wire to the other terminal.

4. Attach the free end of one of the wires connected to the battery to a light socket screw. Connect the other free end of the battery wire to a screw in the wood block.

5. Attach one end of the third wire to the remaining socket terminal. Wrap the other end of the wire around the screw holding the metal strip. Tighten the screw.

6. Bend the free end of the metal strip upward so that it does not make contact with the nearby screw. (See illustration.)

7. Insert the bulb into the socket. You are ready to use your telegraph!

How to Use the Telegraph

The metal strip serves as a switch. When you press the switch to touch the screw beneath it, the circuit is complete (closed circuit), and the light flashes on. When you release the switch, you break the circuit (open circuit) because the metal switch is no longer in contact with the screw. When this happens, the light goes off.

Transmit messages with your telegraph and the Morse code activity on page 37. To make a dot, hold the switch down for a short time. To make a dash, hold the switch down for a longer time. Practice sending messages to a friend.

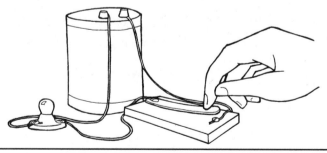

Internet Extender

Early Telegraphs

http://www.chss.montclair.edu/~pererat/perpix.html

Activity Summary: Visit this Web site and follow the links to see pictures of many early telegraphs.

Science

Water and Electricity?

You have probably been reminded not to touch an electric wire while handling an object containing water, because "electricity and water don't mix." Or, you may have been asked to leave a swimming area during an electrical storm. Although purified water (free of conducting materials) acts as an insulator by stopping the flow of electric current, salty or impure water conducts electricity. Try the following experiment and extension to discover how electricity behaves in the presence of water.

Materials: 3 feet (1 meter) insulated wire; 2 batteries connected in series (see illustration), generating about 6 volts of electricity; 3-volt bulb and demonstration light socket; screwdriver; wire strippers; tumbler of warm water; 2 long steel screws; salt

Directions

1. Cut the wire into four pieces as follows: two 12" (30 cm) lengths; one 8" (20 cm) length; one 4" (10 cm) length. Strip the ends of each length of wire.

2. Use a screwdriver to attach the four wires to the socket, screws, and batteries as shown in the illustration below. Be sure that the batteries are connected with positive and negative poles attached correctly.

3. Place the screws into the tumbler of warm water. Do not allow them to touch each other. Does the bulb light up?

4. Take the screws out and add some salt to the water. Place the screws in the water again. Observe what happens.

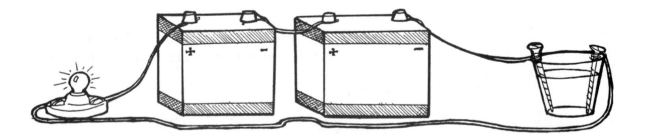

Explanation: When salt is added to the water, it conducts electricity by carrying electrical current from one screw to the other. The current flowing through the water, salt, and screws, causes them to change into other substances. The reaction forces bubbles of hydrogen gas to escape from the water.

Extension: Allow the equipment and connections to remain undisturbed for awhile. What do you think will happen? Write your prediction on the experiment form on page 46. Complete the form as you continue the experiment. Share your results with the class.

Evolution of Light Sources

The light sources listed below were all used at one time. The incandescent light bulb is still used today. Each of these sources had some drawbacks that prevented it from being a constant, reliable light source. Because of the individual problems that each light source presented, new and improved methods evolved. Modern sources of light continue to undergo change and improvement as the need for better and more efficient illumination grows.

Directions: For this activity you will need reference materials about the types of light sources people used throughout history. In a small group, locate information about the light sources below. For each box, list some of the problems (drawbacks) associated with the light source. Research to find dates (approximate in many cases) indicating when the light source was most widely used. On a large piece of construction paper or butcher paper, make a time line on the evolution of the light sources. Make drawings to illustrate the light sources and place them at appropriate places along the time line.

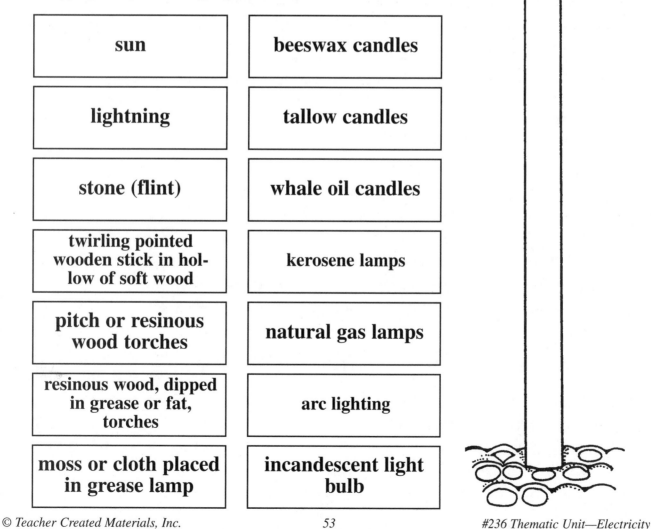

sun	beeswax candles
lightning	tallow candles
stone (flint)	whale oil candles
twirling pointed wooden stick in hollow of soft wood	kerosene lamps
pitch or resinous wood torches	natural gas lamps
resinous wood, dipped in grease or fat, torches	arc lighting
moss or cloth placed in grease lamp	incandescent light bulb

Electricity Scientists and Inventors

Internet Extenders

Directions: Share the "Brief History of Electricity Use" at the Web site shown below with all the students. Assign student groups to investigate the scientists and inventors who were involved in the study and use of electricity. When they complete their research, have the groups work out a system of presenting this information chronologically to the class. They may wish to use a TV talk show format. Encourage them to introduce creativity into their presentations by using costumes, humor, and interesting antidotes about each person.

Brief History of Electricity Use

http://www.bydesign.com/fossilfuels/links/html/electricity/electric_history.html

Summary: Thales of Miletus and Otto von Guericke, who were part of the history of electricity, are briefly mentioned in this interesting information.

Scientist/Inventors

http://www.ideafinder.com/facts/fip.htm

Summary: The following scientists and inventors are found at this Web site.

Guglielmo Marconi

http://www.ideafinder.com/fact/inventors/marconi.htm

(more information at this Web site: http://www.marconiusa.org/marconi/index.html)

Nikola Tesla

http://www.ideafinder.com/facts/inventors/tesla.htm

Heinrich Hertz

http://www.ideafinder.com/facts/inventors/hertz.htm

Count Alessandro Volta

http://etabeta.unipv.it/volta1999

Hans Christian Oersted, Andre Marie Ampere, William Gilbert

http://www.english.upenn.edu/%7Ejlynch/FrankDemo/People/oersted.htm

George Simon Ohm

http://www.english.upenn.edu/%7jlynch/FrankDemo/People/ohm.htm

Joseph Henry

http://www.si.edu/archives/ihd/jhp/

Great Discoveries in Electricity

The Discovery Cards on pages 56 and 57 provide dates and information about great discoveries in the study of electricity. The Scientist/Inventor Cards on pages 58 and 59 contain the names of the scientists and inventors responsible for those discoveries.

Directions

- Divide the class into groups of two.

- Reproduce enough copies of pages 56-59 so that each group has a set. Have students cut out the cards on these pages.

- Ask students to read the cards to learn which scientist or inventor is credited with which discovery by matching the numbered cards. Encourage them to practice matching the scientist or inventor with the discovery.

- When student pairs are ready, have them play a "Great Discoveries Match-up Game" using the following rules:

  1. Place all cards face down on a playing surface. (If you wish to play with fewer match-up cards, choose an equal number of discovery cards and matching scientist/inventor cards. Put the remaining cards aside.)

  2. Decide which player will start the game. Player 1 chooses two cards. If the player does not choose a matching Discovery Card and the Scientist/Inventor Card, he or she turns the cards face down again. If the cards match, the player keeps them. Player 2 continues in the same way. The game is over when all cards have been matched. The player with the greatest number of matching cards is the winner.

1 *600 B.C.*
discovers attractive power of charged amber
(Greek scientist and philosopher)

7 *Benjamin Franklin*

20 *Guglielmo Marconi*

12 *1827*
discovers the relation between current voltage, and resistance in an electric circuit
(German physicist)

Extension: Have students cut out the cards on pages 56-59 and use scientists/inventors and their discoveries to create a time line. Use a large piece of construction paper or butcher paper for the background of the time line. Glue the cards to the appropriate areas of the time line. Students can decorate their time lines with pictures of the discoveries.

Discovery Cards

See page 55 for directions.

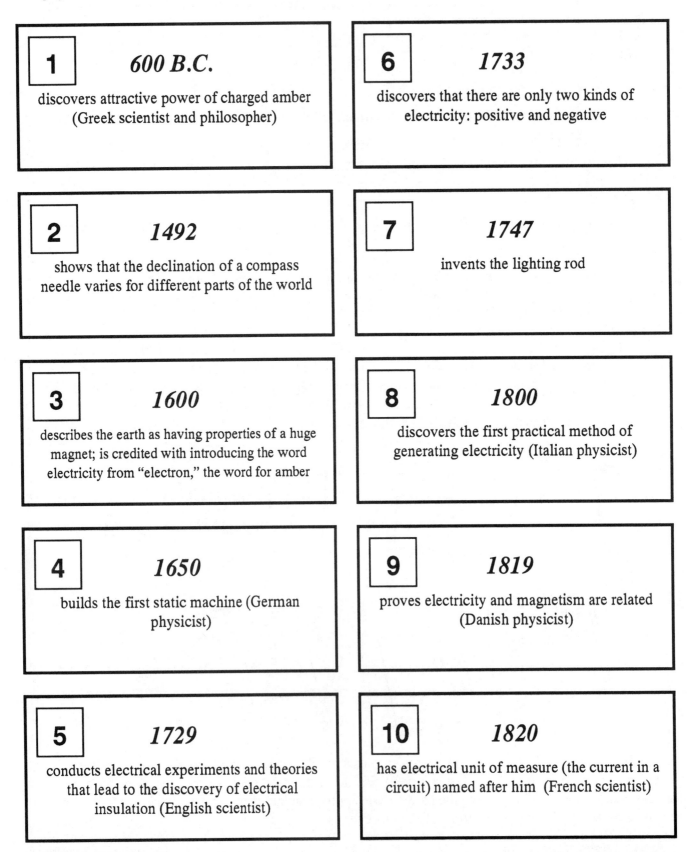

1	**600 B.C.**

discovers attractive power of charged amber (Greek scientist and philosopher)

2	**1492**

shows that the declination of a compass needle varies for different parts of the world

3	**1600**

describes the earth as having properties of a huge magnet; is credited with introducing the word electricity from "electron," the word for amber

4	**1650**

builds the first static machine (German physicist)

5	**1729**

conducts electrical experiments and theories that lead to the discovery of electrical insulation (English scientist)

6	**1733**

discovers that there are only two kinds of electricity: positive and negative

7	**1747**

invents the lighting rod

8	**1800**

discovers the first practical method of generating electricity (Italian physicist)

9	**1819**

proves electricity and magnetism are related (Danish physicist)

10	**1820**

has electrical unit of measure (the current in a circuit) named after him (French scientist)

56

Discovery Cards *(cont.)*

See page 55 for directions.

11   *1821*

experiments with currents produced by magnetism (English chemist and physicist)

16   *1875*

develops the electric telephone

12   *1827*

discovers the relation between current voltage, and resistance in an electric circuit (German physicist)

17   *1879*

develops the light bulb

13   *1831*

builds the first electromagnet (American inventor)

18   *1888*

discovers that electricity may be transmitted by electromagnetic waves

14   *1840*

invents telegraph

19   *1888*

discovers alternating current

15   *1859*

makes first lead-acid storage cell to store electricity (French inventor)

20   *1895*

begins experiments with "wireless telegraphy" (radio)

Scientist/Inventor Cards

See page 55 for directions.

1 **_Thales of Miletus_**

2 **_Christopher Columbus_**

3 **_William Gilbert_**

4 **_Otto van Guericke_**

5 **_Stephan Gray_**

6 **_Charles Francois de Cisternay Du Fay_**

7 **_Benjamin Franklin_**

8 **_Alessandro Volta_**

9 **_Hans Christian Oersted_**

10 **_Andre Marie Ampere_**

Scientist/Inventor Cards *(cont.)*

See page 55 for directions.

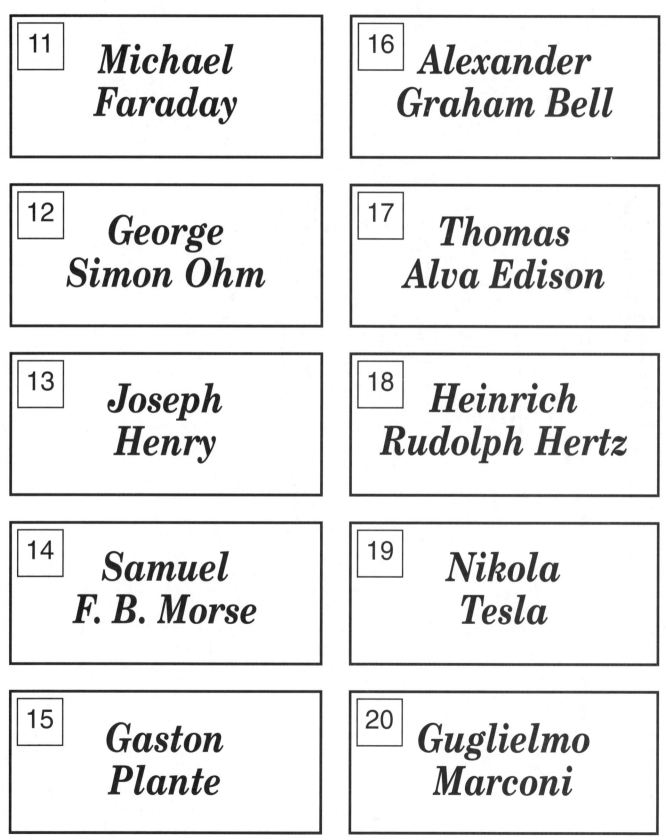

11 Michael Faraday	**16** Alexander Graham Bell
12 George Simon Ohm	**17** Thomas Alva Edison
13 Joseph Henry	**18** Heinrich Rudolph Hertz
14 Samuel F. B. Morse	**19** Nikola Tesla
15 Gaston Plante	**20** Guglielmo Marconi

United States Map

Directions: On the map below, show the locations of major nuclear power plants and the major hydroelectric plants. Make a key.

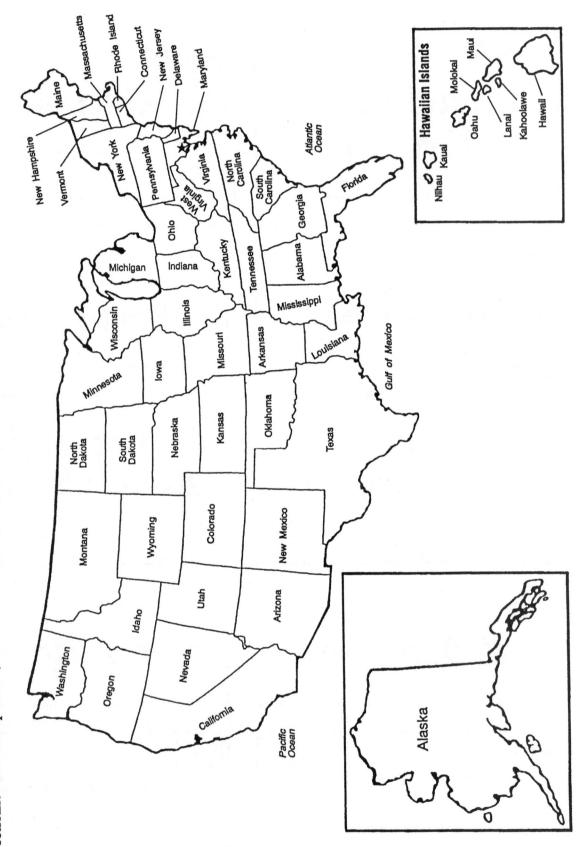

World Map

Directions: There are many countries in the world that are still considered primitive. They are just beginning to use electricity as a source of power. On the map below, indicate the major hydroelectric plants throughout the world.

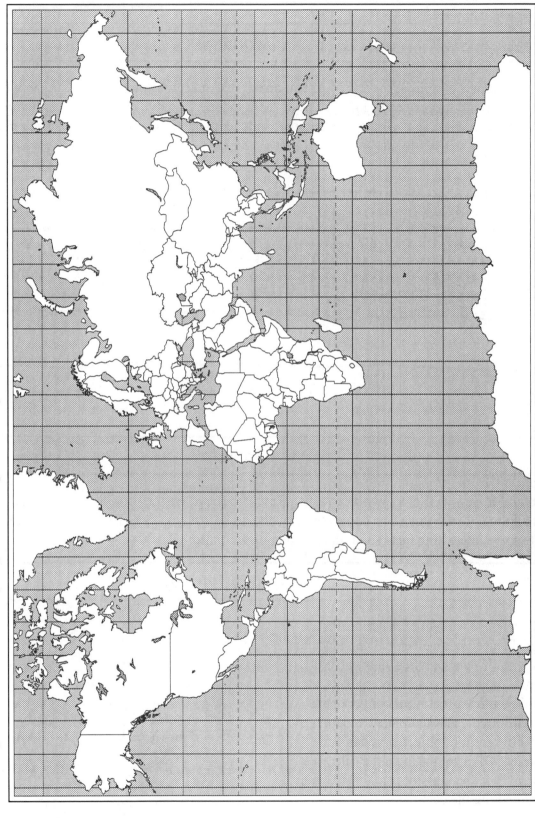

Art Projects

| *Montage* |

Collect pictures of appliances and other equipment that are run by electricity. Cut them out of newspapers and magazines and glue or paste them to letters you've cut out of construction paper, spelling ELECTRICITY. Attach the letters to butcher paper or an old sheet to use as a banner.

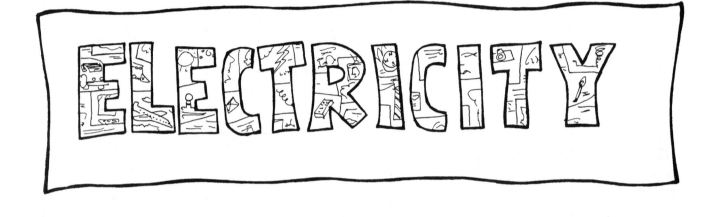

| *Copy Art* |

Samuel Morse was first known as an artist. Research in Art History books to find some of his paintings or sculpture. Make your own copies of his works as best as you can. Below each recreated piece of art, write some interesting facts about the painting or sculpture.

| *Electrical Parts Art* |

Collect an assortment of materials that might be used in an electrical appliance or machine. Washers, wires, nuts and bolts, screws, old switch plates and sockets, etc. Build your own sculpture from the parts you collected. The sculpture can represent a specific form or object, or it can be abstract. Give your sculpture a title. Display it in the classroom and share your creation with the class.

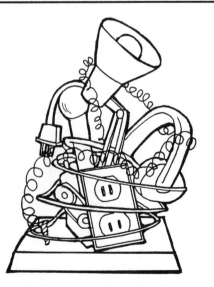

62

Home Sweet Home

Directions: If you could design the interior of a modern home, what would it look like? Using the floor plan below, decide what furnishings and electrical appliances you might include. Cut out pictures in newspapers or magazines, or draw and color appropriate furniture and appliances to fit this modern home. Add labels where necessary. Consider the placement, electrical safety factors, and usage of appliances as you design each room. Share your floor plan with the class.

Extension: Use the information on pages 41-42 to determine whether or not a circuit would overload in any one room if all appliances in that room were used at the same time.

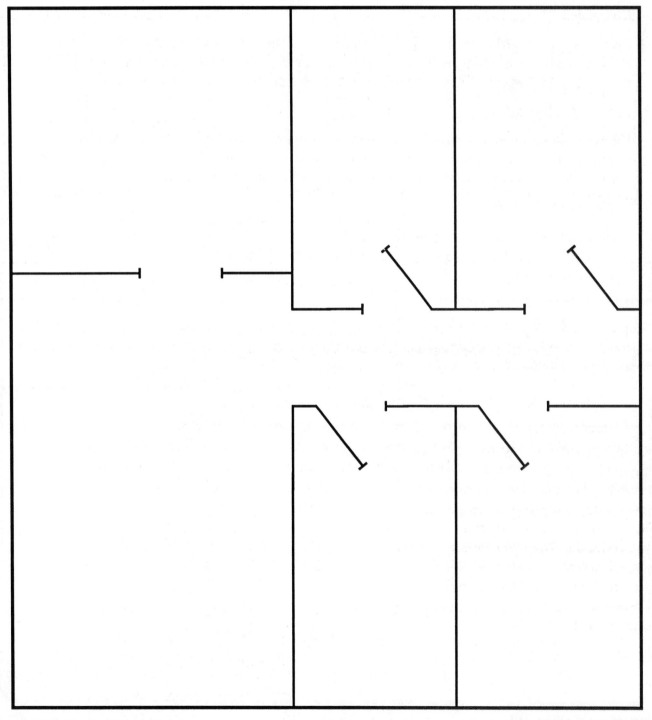

Careers

Directions: Careers in the field of electricity are many and varied. Since the beginning of the Age of Electricity more opportunities developed as new inventions were unveiled. Some of the career possibilities available today are presented below. Read each description. Then, research one of the occupations listed or learn about one of your own choosing. On a separate piece of paper, write why you might choose that particular one as a career. Describe the education and skills you might need to succeed in that career choice, how you would go about getting hired for it, the duties involved, and any goals you have.

Electrician

Electricians put together and install electrical systems. They follow wiring diagrams to install electrical equipment, wiring, and communication systems. Electricians join wires and connect them to circuit breakers. They must be sure that their work follows local building rules.

Electrical Line Maintainer

Electrical line maintainers make and repair the lines that carry electricity from power plants to electricity users. They climb poles to install transformers and other electrical equipment. They install wires between poles and may also fix broken wires or other damaged equipment.

Maintenance Electrician

Maintenance electricians fix electrical equipment and make sure it runs smoothly. They work with equipment such as motors, switches, transformers, wiring, and alarm systems. They work in manufacturing industries.

Electric Motor Technician

Electric motor technicians fix electric generators, motor starters, and related equipment. Technicians take motors apart and decide whether parts should be repaired or replaced. Most technicians work in repair shops or service centers.

Electrical Appliance Technician

Electrical appliance technicians fix small and large household appliances. These include toasters, mixers, washers, ranges, and refrigerators. Appliance technicians work for appliance stores and repair shops, or service centers. They may work in the shop or in customers' homes and businesses.

Electrical Engineer

Electrical engineers design, develop, test, and supervise the manufacture of electrical equipment, including power generating and transmission equipment, electric motors, machinery controls, lighting, and wiring in buildings.

Electric Power Generating Plant Operators

These operators control the machinery that generates electricity. Operators regulate and monitor boilers, turbines, generators, auxiliary equipment, switching gears, and nuclear reactors used to generate electricity from a central control room.

Candles As a Light Source

Before electricity was harnessed and the light bulb was invented, people experimented with many different materials to illuminate their homes. Kitchen fats and drippings from the various meats that people ate such as hogs, cows, sheep, bears, and poultry were used. Tallow (the hard fatty tissue or suet of sheep, cattle, etc.) was heated until the melting separated the fibrous and membranous matter from the fat. Then, lengths of cotton wick hung from a rod were dipped repeatedly into the molten fat until the candle shape formed. This became a popular and inexpensive method of making candles.

Although the invention of the molded candle in the eighteenth century increased candle production, dipped candles still produced a cleaner, brighter, and more even light.

Share the following candle-dipping experience with the class.

Materials: box of paraffin wax; 2 coffee cans; hot plate or stove; candle wicking or string; crayon bits for color; pot larger than coffee cans; water; potholders or oven mitts; dowels or long pencils

Preparation

1. Heat water in a large pot. The water level should be lower than the top of a coffee can.

2. Put the paraffin slab into an empty coffee can. (Add crayon bits for color if desired.) Carefully place the can into the pot of hot water. Allow the wax to melt. Warm wax produces a better candle than hot wax.

3. Prepare the wick by cutting a length of string twice the depth of the can (about 12"/30 cm for a double candle and 6"/15 cm for a single candle).

4. Fill a second coffee can with ice water.

Directions: Hold the wick for the double candle in the center, dipping it into wax and then into cold water. Straighten the wick after each cold water dip. Continue this procedure until the candle "grows" to the desired size. If making a single candle, tie the wick to a pencil or stick before beginning to dip it. This will avoid the possibility of burning fingers.

Hang the candles from a coat hanger to cool and harden. (Wicks of the double candles can be hung over the bottom of wire hangers; single candles can be attached by the wicks using a clothespin.) Cut the double candles apart. Display the candles around the room.

Caution: Never allow children to work unsupervised. Paraffin is dangerous. Never boil, overheat, or mix with water. It should only be melted in a double boiler. Wax can ignite and smoke. (Wax fires must be smothered. Treat hot wax just as you would hot oil.)

Public Hearings

Electric companies serve the public. As a result, people want to know how the electric company runs its business. If a new electric plant is needed in an area, representatives from the company go to the energy agency in that region. The agency holds public hearings. At public hearings, individuals who are in favor of the electric plant tell why the plant should be built. Speakers who are opposed explain why it should not be built. Anyone can go to these hearings, listen to the arguments for or against the issues, and make up his or her own mind. On a given date, a vote is taken to decide whether or not the plant will be constructed on the proposed site.

Hold a Mock Public Hearing

- Break up into 2 groups after deciding what type of power plant your mock electric company wants to build.

- Assign one group to be in favor of the power plant. The other group will oppose the building of the plant.

- The groups should brainstorm ideas about the points they would like to make in support of their positions on the issue. Each group should then elect a spokesperson to represent it at the hearing.

- The group supporting the electric company proposal should include some of these ideas and preparations: draw up plans; tell why the new plant is needed; explain why one type of plant would be better for the area; give cost savings to the consumer; be environmentally safe.

- The consumer group opposing the plant site could consider such topics for argument as: the impact on the environment; the possible hidden cost to the community; the negative effects on community life.

- Both groups will need sensible reasons to support their statements. When arguing a point of view on any topic, factual information based on research provides strong support. Locate and keep notes on information you have found that will support your point of view.

- Elect someone to be the chairperson of the meeting, to make sure the hearing runs smoothly and everyone gets a fair chance to speak. The rest of the class will be in the audience. Try to listen objectively to both sides as they present their side. Then have a mock election to vote on this issue.

You may choose to use the ballot below for your election or create a ballot form of your own.

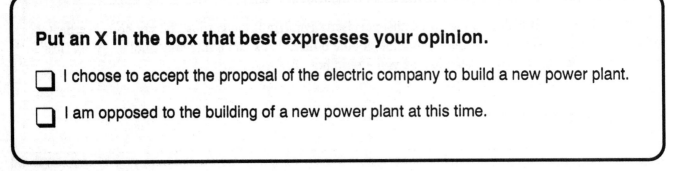

Put an X in the box that best expresses your opinion.

☐ I choose to accept the proposal of the electric company to build a new power plant.

☐ I am opposed to the building of a new power plant at this time.

A Day Without Electricity

We all tend to take electricity for granted. We are so used to having the conveniences offered by electricity, that when the power goes off, we forget and try to use our electrical items anyway.

Plan a day in your classroom to be electricity-free (as practical as possible). Tape paper over light switches and outlets, unplug computers, overhead projectors, TV, intercoms, etc. Pack a sack lunch for the day and eat in the room.

If possible, try a day (or a few hours) without electricity at home. You will need the help and cooperation of your family. This activity should prove to be an interesting and unusual experience for everyone.

When you have completed the activity, use the space below to write your thoughts about what a day without electricity was like. Share your experiences with the class.

A Day in the Dark

_____

_____

_____

_____

_____

_____

_____

_____

_____

_____

_____

_____

_____

_____

_____

_____

_____

Electricity Fair

Set aside a day to have an "Electricity Fair." Invite another class, parents and relatives, senior citizen groups, etc., to view the many projects and displays completed while studying this unit.

- Set up booths or centers to display the science projects. In addition to the curriculum activities presented in the unit, you may wish to add a center that includes projects or experiments on electricity that the students have done. (See the next activity for a possible student project to demonstrate.) Have students demonstrate the experiments and be ready to answer any questions. Invite visitors to try out the experiments.

- Have student groups use the information on pages 69–71 to make turbines and to discover how a turbine works to generate electricity. You may wish to display the turbines during the "Electricity Fair." Ask group members to explain how the turbines work.

- Display math papers, art projects, Venn diagrams, language arts activities, and time lines around the room. Have students read papers they have written from "Daily Writing Topics."

- Enlarge social studies maps to display power plants in the United States and around the world.

- In the classroom, set up an observation table that includes completed student projects and equipment for experimenting with electricity and magnetism. Students and guests will have opportunities for real-life science experiences. For example, small electric motors, circuit breakers, and simple crystal radio sets can provide vehicles for discovery learning. Allow time during the fair for students and visitors to work with the materials provided. If possible, provide related books at the observation table to be used for reference. As students and visitors use the observation area, expect to hear stimulating conversations and interesting questions arise.

Electricity Observation Table

Build a Turbine

Have student groups complete the following group project. The turbines can be displayed at the "Electricity Fair" (see page 68.)

Prepare for the activity by asking students to think about the following questions:

Where does the electricity that we use come from?

Have you ever heard of a turbine?

Explain that in the following activity students will make a turbine and learn how it works to produce electricity. Discuss power plants and how they operate. (See page 70 for background information.)

Divide the class into small groups. Distribute the materials listed below and have students follow the directions to complete their turbines. When all projects are finished, compare the turbines made in class to a generator's turbine. Can the basic principle of the class turbines be expanded to show how an electrical generator works? Discuss student responses. (Refer to the information on page 70, if necessary.)

Materials

- piece of cardboard
- turbine patterns, one per group (page 71)
- tape
- two thumbtacks
- scissors
- pencil
- long thin nail
- two paper clips
- wood block

Directions to students

1. Cut out the turbine pattern.
2. Carefully poke a long thin nail through its center.
3. Secure it with tape and twist each blade slightly inward.
4. Bend two paper clips and tack them into the wooden block as shown in the diagram.
5. Place the ends of the nail into the paper clip cradles.
6. Blow on your turbine.

Adapted from TCM #646

Build a Turbine *(cont.)*

Background Information

Read the following information to find out more about power plants and the role of the turbine in the production of electricity.

- The electricity used in homes and industry is generated at man-made power stations. There are three main types of power stations that generate electricity. One type uses fast flowing water to turn the turbines. The second and most common type uses oil or coal to generate steam that runs the turbines. The third type of power station uses nuclear energy.

- The basic premise is that turbines are turned to power an electrical generator. The electrical generator spins a magnet between coils of wire. The bigger the magnet and coils, the greater the voltage output. If the magnet spins faster, there will also be an increase in the voltage.

- The power stations generate the electricity at about 11,000 volts. This is not a high enough voltage to deliver the electricity economically. Therefore, the electricity is sent through a transformer and stepped up to 400,000 volts. Then the electricity is carried over the wires. This voltage is far too high for a house or business. When it reaches an area substation, it is stepped down through another transformer. This lower voltage is then carried to homes and businesses.

- The voltage coming into a home is very high. It has enough power to kill a person. Playing with plugs and sockets is very dangerous.

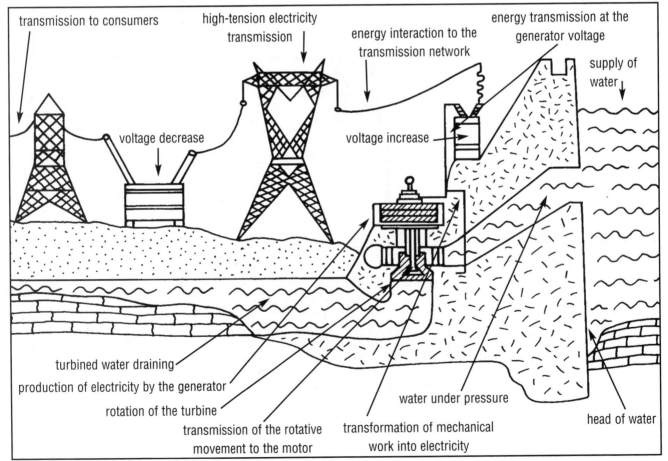

Adapted from TCM #646

Build a Turbine *(cont.)*

Cut out the turbine pattern.

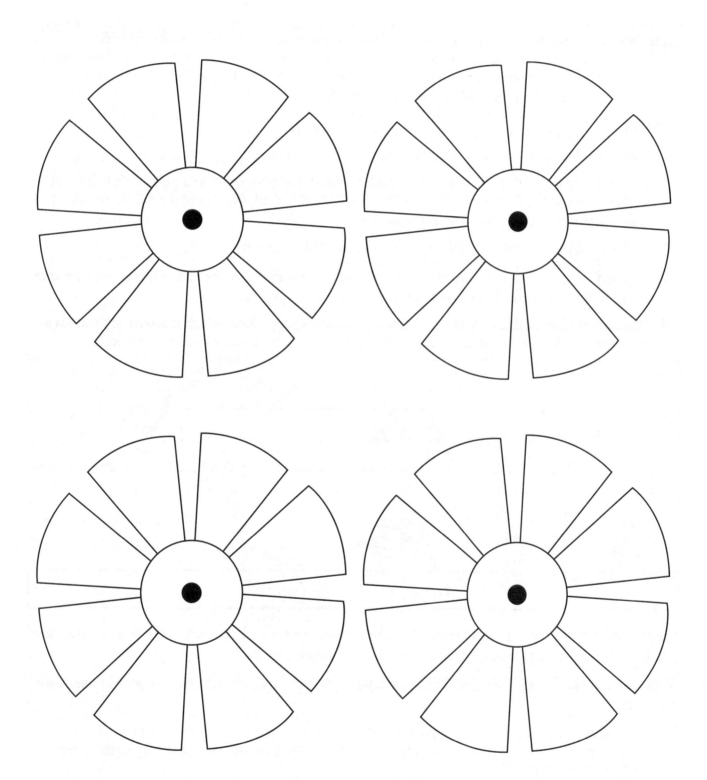

Adapted from TCM #646

#236 Thematic Unit—Electricity

Steady As It Goes!

Build the following game board and test your skill at holding a steady hand as you play "Steady As It Goes!"

Materials: 1.5-volt dry cell; 3 feet (1 meter) of thin insulated wire; 1 foot (.3 meters) of stiff, irregularly-shaped bare wire; 6" (15 cm) of stiff straight wire with small loop at one end; 2 small nails; demonstration flashlight socket and bulb; small board (approximately 12"/30 cm) long for mounting game; screwdriver; hammer

Directions

1. Divide the insulated wire into three equal pieces. Strip the ends of each piece of wire.

2. Attach a wire to one dry cell terminal. Attach the other end of the wire to a light socket terminal. Attach a second wire to the other dry cell terminal. Secure the loose end of the wire to the small board with a nail. Label this connection point A.

3. Drive a nail into the opposite end of the board and label it point B.

4. Connect the third wire to the other end of light socket. Attach the loose end of this wire to the wire with the small loop on the end, as shown.

5. Place the stiff, irregularly-shaped wire through the small loop. Now attach this wire to the nails at points A and B. (This wire should rest above the board so the small wire loop can pass freely over the wire.)

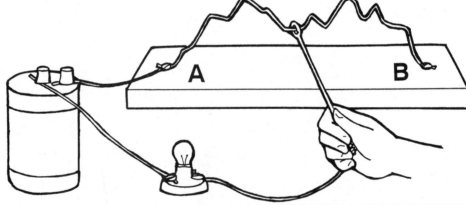

How To Play the Game

Start the loop at A. Try to go to B without touching the bare wire. If you touch it, the bulb lights up and you lose. Have a contest to see who has steady hands. Good Luck!

Note: As you become more skilled at this game, you may wish to change the rules of play to one of the following:

1. Start at point A and move toward point B without causing the bulb to light. The player who reaches point B successfully, or the player who travels the greatest distance before lighting the bulb, is the winner.

2. Start at point A and move toward point B as quickly as you can without touching the bare wire. The player who reaches point B in the shortest amount of time is the winner.

72

Bulletin Board Ideas

Attracting Your Attention

Reproduce and cut out the clip art pattern on page 74. Have students bring in photographs (or draw self-portraits) of themselves to place inside the magnet. Staple some of the students' magnets to a bulletin board titled "Attracting Your Attention." Surround the students' magnets with samples of their work. Each week, feature another group of students and their work.

Featuring Thomas Alva Edison

Reproduce the portrait of Thomas Edison on page 76 and the battery and light bulb socket on page 75. Place the portrait in the center of a bulletin board. (Depending on the size of the bulletin board you will use, you may wish to enlarge it.) Have students prepare illustrations and information about some of the highlights and accomplishments of Edison's life. Glue each picture or sheet of information to a colorful piece of construction paper. Display the pieces of construction paper on the bulletin board. Use yarn to connect each to the portrait, as shown. Coil yarn around the edge of the bulletin board, twisting it to resemble coiled wire. Attach the border of yarn to the battery clip art and two or more light bulb sockets. (See illustration.)

We're Getting Brighter

Make a pictograph to show the number of books students read about inventors or scientists and other topics related to electricity. Reproduce and cut out several copies of the light bulb pattern on page 33 (shrink it to the appropriate size in a copy machine). Write the names of each student on the graph. Place one light bulb on the pictograph for each book a student has read.

Clip Art

See page 73 for directions.

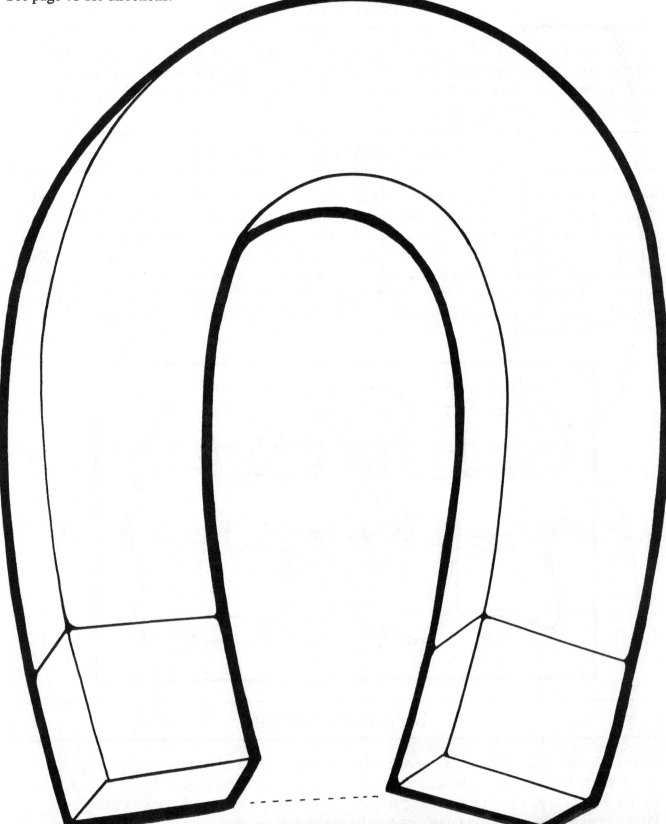

74

Clip Art *(cont.)*

See page 73 for directions.

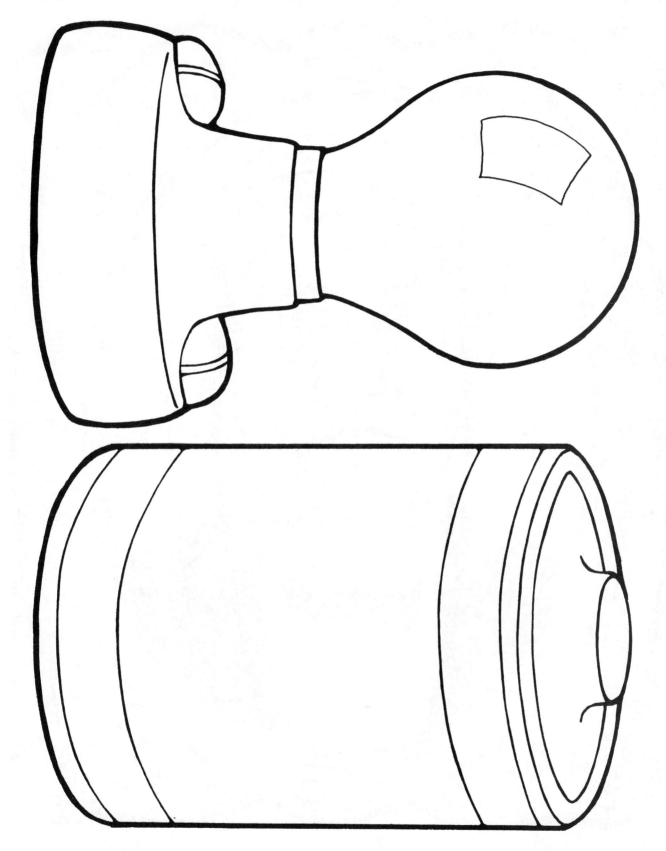

Clip Art *(cont.)*

See page 73 for directions.

Safety Rules

Experimenting with electricity can be lots of fun, but if used improperly or carelessly, electricity can be very dangerous. Here are some important rules to remember when working around or with electricity. Read and discuss them with your friends and family. Then, add your own safety rules about electricity.

- Never touch an electrical appliance or switch with wet hands.

- Before plugging or unplugging an electrical appliance, make sure the power is turned off.

- When connecting or disconnecting an electrical device, be sure it is unplugged.

- If an electrical cord is worn, do not use it. Tell an adult that it needs to be replaced.

- Do not overload a circuit by plugging in too many electrical appliances at one time.

- Remove the batteries from toys and games when they are not being used for a long time. An old, corroded battery left in a toy or game can destroy it.

- Do not touch a bare wire.

- Never handle an electrical appliance, switch, telephone set, or radio while in the bathtub.

_____

_____

_____

_____

_____

_____

_____

Awards

Congratulations

_____

(Student's Name)

**Your Work
Has Been**

Electrifying

_____

Teacher's Signature

Superscientist
Award

Presented to

_____

(Student's Name)

for _____

_____

(Teacher's Signature)

Bibliography

Aaseng, Nathan. *The Inventors: Nobel Prizes in Chemistry, Physics, and Medicine.* Lerner LB, 1987

Arco. Energy, *Forces and Resources.* Arco, 1984

Ardley, Neil. *Science Book of Electricity.* Harcourt Brace, 1991

Ardley, Neil. *Exploring Magnetism.* Watts LB, 1984

Asimov, Isaac. *Asimov's Biographical Encyclopedia of Science and Technology.* Doubleday, 1982

Asimov, Isaac. *How Did We Find Out About Superconductivity?* Walker LB, 1988

Baker, Wendy. *Haslam Electricity: A Creative, Hands on Approach to Science*, Aladdin, 1993

Boltz, C.L. *How Electricity Is Made.* Facts On File, 1985

Bronowski, J, and Millicent E. Selsam. *Biography of an Atom.* Harper Collins, 1987

Challonor, Jack. *My First Batteries and Magnets Book*, Dorling Kindersley, 1992

Cosner, Shaaron. *The Light Bulb.* Walker & Co., 1984

Dunn, Andrew. *It's Electric.* Thomson Learning, 1993

Fricke, Pam. *Careers with an Electric Company.* Lerner, 1984

Friedhoffer, Robert. *Magnetism and Electricity.* Watts, 1992

Gibson, Gary. *Kenyon's Understanding Electricity (Science for Fun).* Copper Beech Books, 1995

Gutnik, Martin. *Electricity: From Faraday to Solar Generators.* Franklin Watts, 1986

Gutnik, Martin. *Michael Faraday, Creative Scientist.* Childrens Press, 1986

Gutnik, Martin. *Simple Electrical Devices.* Franklin Watts, 1986

Halacy, Dan. *Nuclear Energy.* Watts, 1984

Kerrodd, Robin. *Future Energy and Resources.* (*Today's World*) Gloucester Press, 1990

Lambert, Mark. *Future Sources of Energy.* Watts, 1986

Lampton, Christopher. *Thomas Alva Edison.* Grey Castle Press, 1991

Lewis, Cynthia Copeland. *Hello, Alexander Graham Bell Speaking: A Biography.* Dillon Press, 1991

McKie, Robin. *Energy.* Hampstead LB, 1989

McKie, Robin. *Solar Power.* Gloucester, 1985

Quackenbush, Robert. *Quick, Annie, Give Me a Catchy Line! A Story of Samuel F.B. Morse.* Prentice Hall, 1983

Parker, Steve. *Electricity.* (Eyewitness-Science) Dorling Kindersley, Inc., 1992

Parker, Steve. *Thomas Edison and Electricity.* Chelsea House, 1995

Parsons, Alexandra. *Electricity.* (Make-It-Work!, Science) Thomson Learning, 1995

Peacock, Graham. *Electricity.* Thomson Learning, 1993

Richards, Norman. *Dreamers and Doers: Inventors Who Changed the World.* Macmillan, 1984

Roberts, Royston M. *Serendipity-Accidental Discoveries in Science.* John Wiley & Sons, Inc., 1989

Strachan, James. *Future Sources.* Gloucester, 1985

Whyman, Kathryn. *Electricity & Magnetism.* Gloucester, 1986

Whyman, Kathryn. *Sparks to Power Station.* Gloucester, 1989

Wood, Robert W. *Physics for Kids.* Tab Books, 1990

Answer Key

Page 21

A. 444	I. 745	R. 441
C. 672	K. 240	S. 27
D. 45	L. 380	T. 44
E. 211	M. 29	U. 248
G. 106	N. 365	W. 457
H. 17	O. 153	Y. 122

Energy Facts: 1. motion; 2. kinetic; 3. Wind; 4. energy; 5. Heat; 6. Sound; 7. Electricity; 8. changed

Page 24

1. B	3. G	5. J	7. D	9. I
2. E	4. A	6. H	8. F	10. C

Page 36

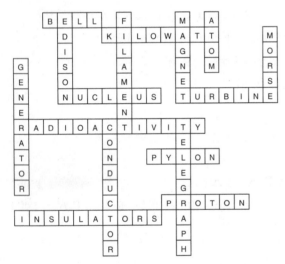

Page 38

1. 1895	4. 120	7. 1,000
2. 1975	5. 15	8. 437
3. 2,000	6. 20	9. 15

Page 39

Ted's house—May: 5,890

Ted's house—June: 6,539

Mary's house—May: 3,295

Mary's house—June: 4,444

1. 649
2. 1,149
3. Mary's
4. 500

Page 40

Kilowatt Questions: 1=January; 2=July; 3=June, July, September

Calculator Corners: January=$5; February=$4.75; March=$4.50; April= $4.00; May=$3.75; June=$3.75; July=$2.50; August=$4.50; September=$3.75; October=$4.25; November=$4.25; December=$4.75

Page 41

air conditioner=12; blender=2; can opener=1; coffee maker=5; dryer= 55; freezer=3; iron=9; floor lamp=3; mixer=1; electric range=109; refrigerator=2; television=3; toaster=1; vacuum cleaner=4; washing machine=3

Questions: 1. dryer, electric range; 2. dryer, electric range; They use heat.

Page 42

Total Amperes: Circuit 1=23; Circuit 2=12; Circuit 3=10; Circuit 4=27

Questions: 1. Circuit 2 and 3; 2. Answers will vary.; 3. Circuit 3

Page 43

air conditioner=5000 W, 45.5 AMPS; dishwasher=1804 W, 1.8 KW; food warmer= .5 KW, 4.5 AMPS; fryer=1320 W, 13 KW; furnace=300 W, 2.7 AMPS; garbage disposer= 9. KW, 8.2 AMPS; grill=1300 W, 11.8 AMPS; hot water heater=2.5 KW, 22.7 AMPS; sun lamp=275 W, .3 KW

Questions: 1.6 items; 2. food warmer, fryer, furnace, garbage disposer, grill, sun lamp